KT-197-275

ONE WEEK LOAN

AUSTRALIA
Lawbook Co.
Sydney

CANADA and USA
Carswell
Toronto

HONG KONG
Sweet & Maxwell Asia

NEW ZEALAND
Brookers
Wellington

SINGAPORE and MALAYSIA
Sweet & Maxwell Asia
Singapore and Kuala Lumpur

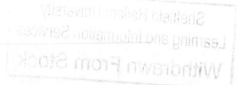

JUDICIAL ACTIVISM
Authority, Principle and Policy in the Judicial Method

by

THE HON JUSTICE MICHAEL KIRBY
AC CMG
Justice of the High Court of Australia

Published under the auspices of
THE HAMLYN TRUST

LONDON
SWEET & MAXWELL
2004

Published in 2004 by *Sweet & Maxwell Limited* of
100 Avenue Road, Swiss Cottage,
London NW3 3PF
Typeset by LBJ Typesetting Ltd of Kingsclere
Printed in Wales by Creative Print and Design Group

No natural forests were destroyed to make this product;
only farmed timber was used and replanted

A CIP catalogue record for this book is available from the British Library

ISBN 0421 879505 (HB)
0421 878300 (PB)

For Johan van Vloten

The above illustration is the work of Sturt Krygsman and was first published in *The Australian* newspaper, October 15, 2003. It is reproduced by permission of the artist and the original is now in the possession of the author.

TABLE OF CONTENTS

THE HAMLYN LECTURES

The Hamlyn Lectures

The Hamlyn Lectures

THE HAMLYN TRUST

The Hamlyn Trust owes its existence to the will of the late Miss Emma Warburton Hamlyn of Torquay, who died in 1941 at the age of 80. She came of an old and well-known Devon family. Her father, William Bussell Hamlyn, practised in Torquay as a solicitor and J.P. for many years, and it seems likely that Miss Hamlyn founded the trust in his memory. Emma Hamlyn was a woman of strong character, intelligent and cultured, well-versed in literature, music and art, and a lover of her country. She travelled extensively in Europe and Egypt, and apparently took considerable interest in the law and ethnology of the countries and cultures that she visited. An account of Miss Hamlyn by Dr Chantal Stebbings of the University of Exeter may be found, under the title "The Hamlyn Legacy", in volume 42 of the published lectures.

Miss Hamlyn bequeathed the residue of her estate on trust in terms which it seems were her own. The wording was thought to be vague, and the will was taken to the Chancery Division of the High Court, which in November 1948 approved a Scheme for the administration of the trust. Paragraph 3 of the Scheme, which closely follows Miss Hamlyn's own wording, is as follows:

> "The object of the charity is the furtherance by lectures or otherwise among the Common People of the United Kingdom of Great Britain and Northern Ireland of the knowledge of the Comparative Jurisprudence and Ethnology of the Chief European countries including the United Kingdom, and the circumstances of the growth of such jurisprudence to the Intent that the Common People of the United Kingdom may realise the privileges which in law and custom they enjoy in comparison with other European Peoples and realising and appreciating such privileges may recognise the responsibilities and obligations attaching to them."

The Trustees are to include the Vice-Chancellor of the University of Exeter, representatives of the Universities of London, Leeds, Glasgow, Belfast and Wales and persons co-opted. At present there are eight Trustees:

From the outset it was decided that the objects of the Trust could best be achieved by means of an annual course of public lectures of outstanding interest and quality by eminent Lecturers, and by their subsequent publication and distribution to a wider audience. The first of the Lectures were delivered by the Rt Hon. Lord Justice Denning (as he then was) in 1949. Since then there has been an unbroken series of annual Lectures. A complete list of the Lectures may be found on pages ix to xii. The Trustees have also, from time to time, provided financial support for a variety of projects which, in various ways, have disseminated knowledge or have promoted a wider public understanding of the law.

The 55th series of lectures was delivered by the Hon. Justice Michael Kirby, at Exeter University and Cardiff Law School, during November 2003. The Board of Trustees would like to record its appreciation to Justice Kirby and also the two University law schools, which generously hosted these lectures.

March 2004   **BARRY A.K. RIDER**
                                        Chairman of the Trustees

PREFACE

The first Hamlyn lectures were given by Lord Denning in 1949. He came to Australia about a decade afterwards, when I was at university. In brilliant addresses he reminded us of the capacity and duty of the common law to develop and adapt to the needs of a changing society. Even as students we knew of his foibles and occasional mistakes. Some of our lecturers complained bitterly about the changes he was making, or proposing, in the law from his influential judicial position.

To most of the young members of the audience, who had not thrown off the idealistic sense that law's mission, concerned with justice, is potentially a noble one, Denning was a breath of fresh air. He signed his photograph which I thrust in front of him. I still have it in my chambers. In later years we corresponded. He demonstrated the truth of what Professor Julius Stone was teaching us in lectures on jurisprudence. Like it or not, judges of the common law have choices. The higher they go the more numerous and more difficult are the leeways for choice. Choice arises in interpreting a written constitution; in construing legislation; and in expressing the principles of the common law and equity for new problems. Denning's was a marvellous message about the capacity and duty of the legal profession to keep the law up to date wherever it could.

Denning's instruction was a notable counterpoint to the lesson that the great Chief Justice of Australia of those days, Sir Owen Dixon, propounded. For Dixon, law would have lost its meaning if the solution to a case did not pre-exist. It would be unworthy of the name of law if it depended on the humour of a judge. For Dixon, "excessive legalism" was a badge of honour. "Strict and complete legalism" was the duty of the law and all of its practitioners. Dixon's recent biography by Philip Ayres shows that he thoroughly disapproved of Denning. Yet Julius Stone argued that the High Court of Australia did not always practise the doctrine that Dixon preached. In Australia, in 1960, Denning seemed a voice for a new era.

The intervening decades, in Australia, the United Kingdom and elsewhere, have seen a continuation of this debate. As Egypt is the gift of the Nile, the common law is the gift of succeeding generations of judges. They cannot avoid their creative function, however much some might like to deny or minimise it. By the last two decades of the twentieth century, in Australia and most other parts of the common law world, judges of great ability accepted Tom Denning's challenge. Perhaps as young lawyers they too had responded to his call.

Judges began to adopt a more transparent methodology. In addition to their primary reliance on legal authority, they came to draw in their decisions upon relevant considerations of legal principle and legal policy. And they would be honest in doing so, not least to themselves. Sometimes, stimulated by written law and sometimes by the common law, they would invoke fundamental principles of human rights. The Old Testament of Dixonian "excessive legalism" began to seem like a breath from a bygone age.

Just at that moment, following a period of exhilarating candour and enlightenment, a Counter-Reformation began. It started about ten years ago and has gathered pace. Its most determined voices have been heard in the United States and Australia; but there were disciples everywhere. As is usually the case in large intellectual movements, there is truth and wisdom in the Counter-Reformation, just as there was in the legal Reformation that preceded it.

Alas, in many places where the common law operates, like zealous converts to the religions of other times and places, the proponents of the competing views came to hurl insults at each other and to denounce the others' methods as lacking in probity: heretical, dishonest and dangerous. Name calling of this kind has attracted, and been stimulated by, political and intellectual bandwagons. They, in turn, have been urged on by the contemporary global media of infotainment, which tends to reduce differences to personalities, party politics and allegations of personal impropriety.

In these lectures, I have set out to explore these divisions and to find some common ground. No judge of integrity can believe that he or she is a free agent, entitled to state the law according to a personal agenda. Yet it is equally wrong to disguise the policy choices that judges must make in performing their functions or to pretend that the pursuit of justice is irrelevant or that words alone, found in past "doctrine", solve all legal problems.

Because the judicial method is central to the performance by judges of their duties, there is no more important debate for the administration of justice. Because the judiciary of the common law has, inescapably, a greater obligation of choice than any other, this is, and always will be, a significant subject for debate and analysis.

Recently, in Sydney, I attended a lecture on the theology of the new Archbishop of Canterbury, Dr Rowan Williams. It followed the controversies surrounding the withdrawal of the nomination as Bishop of Reading of Canon Jeffrey John. Listening to the debate of the theologians, I saw at once reflections of the disputes within the law. There were the strict Biblical constructionists, the verbalists, the traditionalists who resist any change in settled ways. There were those who saw the ever present danger of missing the main point of the entire exercise— whether it is global politics, religion or law. The lecturer helped me see the subjects of these Hamlyn lectures through a lens with a wider focus.

The clashes we have over the judicial method are part of a much broader intellectual conflict characteristic of post modernism. Whilst we must search for common ground, the future of intellectual discourse does not lie in surrendering the truth to an unthinking return to past ways, to past understandings of texts, holy or otherwise, or to forgetting the fundamental mission in which we are engaged. For judges and lawyers, that is a mission of justice according to law. It is not, mechanically, about law alone.

I wish to acknowledge the inspiration I received from my teachers: Tom Denning, Julius Stone and many others. From my family. From colleagues over the years, and from contemporary lawyers, including some of those who now adhere to the doctrines of the Counter-Reformation. We may have arrived at a time, as the Archbishop of Canterbury said in that other context, for a period of quiet reflection, respectful listening and fewer "swear words", such as have marred the contemporary debates about "judicial activism". Certainly, it is well past time for an improvement in community education about the work that judges actually do, and how they do it. A pretence that it is wholly objective, simply verbal and completely policy-free has no place in the relationship between a modern judiciary and the community it serves.

I also acknowledge the assistance I have had in preparing these lectures. The originals were typed by my personal assistant, Janet Saleh. Many materials were presented to me by the librarian of the High Court of Australia, Ms Jacqueline Elliott, and by the Legal Officer to the Court, Mr Alex de Costa. Painstakingly, Mr de Costa helped check the manuscript and correct the final proofs. Useful comments and suggestions were given by my associates (clerks) for 2003: Mr Yane Svetiev, Ms Ully Merkel and Mr Brent Dawkins.

The text of the lectures was written to provide a foundation for their oral presentation. The reference materials are provided to stimulate further debate and perhaps a measure of informed agreement. I took to heart Tom Denning's injunction at the start of his Lectures in 1949. Like Denning, I invited questions and dialogue with my audiences about my views. Some of the points made by my listeners find reflection in the final written text. This, above all, is a subject upon which judges should speak— but also listen.

To the memory of Miss Emma Hamlyn of Torquay, whose bequest made possible the lectures that bear her family name, previous lecturers, the worldwide company of the practitioners of the common law and I will always be grateful.

Michael Kirby
High Court of Australia
Canberra
December 1, 2003.

TABLE OF CASES

Table of Cases

Table of Cases

Table of Cases

Table of Cases

Table of Cases

TABLE OF LEGISLATION

1. Old Testament

INTRODUCTION

A few weeks ago it was spring time in Melbourne. At such a time the High Court of Australia celebrated its first centenary. Exactly a hundred years earlier, Sir Samuel Griffith, Sir Edmund Barton and Richard O'Connor were sworn as the first Justices of the Court. In October 2003, the seven present office-holders entered the Banco Court of the Supreme Court of Victoria to mark the anniversary of that first sitting. I am one of only forty-three judges who have served on the Court. These Hamlyn Lectures are the first by an Australian.

It would have been natural enough to have chosen, as the theme of these lectures, the contributions of the High Court of Australia to the common law that travelled across the oceans to the far side of the world with the soldiers, convicts and settlers who established the British colonies in the Great South Land. The link to the common law of England, and to the judges and lawyers of Britain through the lawbooks, the Privy Council, legal education and personal contacts ensured that Australia remained a child of the common law of England long after settlement and federation. The legacy is still profound. It continues today. I pay a grateful tribute to it.

However, the greatest tribute that can be paid by the children of England's law is to recognise the way in which it helped to rescue them from parochialism,[1] linked them institutionally to one of the world's great legal systems and brought with its books and methodology a unique way of achieving the dual, and sometimes antagonistic, objectives of law: predictable outcomes and individual justice.

If the founding Justices of the High Court of Australia could be with us today, if they went to an airport, a television station

---

[1] F.C.Hutley, "The Legal Traditions of Australia as Contrasted with those of the United States" (1981) 55 *Australian Law Journal* 63, p. 69.

or a modern hospital, learnt of nuclear fission, informatics, space travel and genomics, they would surely be astonished. But if they came down from their portraits and sat in our places for a week, I do not doubt that they would feel immediately at home. The garb would be different, but the foundations of the common law would be familiar. Moreover, the judicial method would seem substantially the same.

In a world of so much change, it therefore seemed inappropriate to limit myself to provincial concerns within my own national borders. Rather unkindly, Miss Hamlyn does not seem to have been much interested in the Empire and Commonwealth when she endowed these lectures. She mentioned comparative jurisprudence of the chief European countries. (Remarkably, she even included the United Kingdom amongst these.) Her omission to refer to the far flung dominions may be proof once again that England established and discarded its Empire (and spread the common law) in a state of absence of mind. Perhaps in the manner of the 1940s, Miss Hamlyn simply looked upon Australians as part of the "Common People of the United Kingdom". She could have been forgiven for so thinking. Many in the settler societies of the Empire at that time looked on themselves in that way.

Like my fellow Antipodean, Lord Cooke of Thorndon, in his lectures,[2] I intend to ignore the call of legal nationalism. Many of my illustrations will come from Australian law because they are the cases I know best. Yet as Lord Cooke pointed out, it is a paradox that the shrinking of the jurisdiction of the Privy Council has actually "promoted the development of the common law". The last two decades have seen not only the growing integration of the law of the United Kingdom with that of the "chief European countries" to which Miss Hamlyn referred so presciently in 1941. They have also witnessed the advance of the "knowledge of the Comparative Jurisprudence" which she also mentioned. There once was a time when lawyers in Commonwealth countries looked mainly, almost wholly, to the law of England. Now we look to each other, to the United States and even to the laws of the European countries. Such is the shrinkage of the world, the expansion of our sources and the enlargement of our imagination and outlook.[3] It is an exciting time to be a lawyer of the common law tradition. Daily the Internet reminds us of our shared treasure. That treasure continues to expand.

[2] Lord Cooke of Thorndon, *Turning Points of the Common Law* (47th Hamlyn Lectures, 1996) (Sweet & Maxwell, London, 1997), p. 2.
[3] *ibid.*, p. 3.

Miss Hamlyn did not want these lectures to be of interest only to judges and lawyers. Faithful to her wishes I have chosen a topic that has attracted popular, as well as professional, concern in all common law countries. I refer to so-called judicial activism. For some, of short memory, judicial activism started when Lord Denning, fresh from his Hamlyn lectures,[4] began to work his changes in the judge-made law. But whenever it first emerged, this is clearly a topic that is, or should be, of interest to ordinary citizens, as Miss Hamlyn hoped her lectures would be. It concerns the way the law of the "Common people" is made. It affects their form of government. It involves the fidelity to their offices of important, well paid and powerful people who sit in the judgment seat. When some of these people are accused of "judicial activism"—even metaphorical "treason" against the constitution[5]—the time has come for ordinary citizens to sit up and pay attention. If the accusation is even partly correct, citizens are entitled to explanations, perhaps even redress. If the accusation is false, that fact should be demonstrated so that the Commons can sleep quietly in their beds.

JUS DICERE NOT *JUS DARE*

Most lawyers of my age, raised in Australia, the United Kingdom or other Commonwealth countries, accepted at the beginning of their journey in the law a rather strict theory about the limits of the power and legitimacy of a common law judge in creating new legal rights or imposing new legal duties on fellow citizens. Occasional judicial remarks might hint that the truth was otherwise.[6] Academics, like Roscoe Pound[7] at Harvard and Julius Stone in Sydney,[8] might teach the scope and obligation of judicial choice. Great cases might be decided, such as

---

[4] Lord Denning, *Freedom Under the Law* (1st ed., Hamlyn Lectures, 1949) (Stevens, London, 1949).

[5] T.Campbell, "Judicial Activism—Justice of Treason?" (2003) 10 *Otago Law Review* 307, p. 314.

[6] *e.g.* Lord Radcliffe, *The Law and Its Compass*, (Rosenthal Lectures, 1960) quoted in R. Stevens, *Law and Politics: The House of Lords as a Judicial Body 1800–1976* (Weidenfeld & Nicolson, London, 1979), p. 620.

[7] R.Pound, *An Introduction to the Philosophy of Law*, (Storrs Lectures on Jurisprudence 1921–2) (Yale University Press, New Haven, 1922). The work of Karl Llewellyn was highly influential later in the 20th century: *The Common Law Tradition: Deciding Appeals* (Little Brown, Boston, 1960) and *The Bramble Bush: On our Law and its Study* (Oceana, New York, 1951); cf. J. Doyle, "Do Judges Make Policy? Should They?" (1998) 57 *Australian Journal of Public Administration* 89, p. 90.

[8] J.Stone, *Province and Function of Law* (Maitland, Sydney, 1946).

Donoghue v Stevenson,[9] which seemed to contradict the strict view. But the fundamental doctrine remained that a judge *applied* the law. A judge did not *make* law.

To this day this simplistic notion is treated as self-evident by many editorialists, not a few politicians and even some disgruntled lawyers. It probably represents the belief about the judicial role shared by many of Miss Hamlyn's "Common people". It taps a reservoir of comfortable verities. It is reinforced by a lack of teaching of civics in the contemporary world and by the din that emanates from the "echo-chamber inhabited by journalists and public moralists".[10] This belief is wrong. Yet part of its survival can be attributed to some very English features of the common law. They have nurtured the mechanical doctrine although the sunlight of truth and reality should long since have dispelled the myths.

Some writers[11] attribute the doctrinal origins of the formalistic theory of common law methodology to the writings of Blackstone. He defined the common law as the ". . . general immemorial custom . . . from time to time declared in the decisions in the courts of justice".[12] There is no doubt that, as a compendious exposition of the common law, published just prior to American independence, Blackstone's classifications had a huge impact on the judicial method, at home but chiefly abroad.

Although there were hints of self-conscious creativity as early as Bracton's writings and in the Year Books,[13] and in the very creation of equity by the Chancellors,[14] the embrace of a limited and fundamentally mechanical conception of the common law judge long predated Blackstone. It was inherent in the role of the Royal judges from the reign of Henry II to enforce the law throughout the Kingdom. This was an attribute of their function as Royal servants. Servants state and apply the law. Making the law is the province of sovereigns.

After the religious Reformation in England in the sixteenth century, the duty of obedient application of the Bible was

---

[9] [1932] A.C. 562.

[10] *Vellino v Chief Constable of the Greater Manchester Police* [2002] 1 W.L.R. 218, *per* Sedley L.J., 233.

[11] *e.g.* M.H.McHugh, "The Law-Making Function of the Judicial Process—Part I" (1988) 62 *Australian Law Journal* 15, pp. 24–25.

[12] W.Blackstone, *Commentaries on the Laws of England* (15th ed, T. Cadell and W. Davies, London, 1809) Vol. 1, p. 73.

[13] W.S.M.Knight, "Public Policy in English Law" (1922) 38 *Law Quarterly Review* 207 at p. 207; P. Parkinson, "Tradition and Change in Legal Reasoning" in P. Parkinson, *Tradition and Change in Australian Law* (2nd ed., LBC, Sydney, 2001) 177, p. 191.

[14] A.F.Mason, "Foreword" in *The Principles of Equity*, (P. Parkinson ed., 2nd ed., LBC, Sydney, 2003), p. v.

sometimes seen as a kind of English antidote to the pretensions to power and broad discretions (perceived features of the old religion). Thus Francis Bacon in one of his essays remarked:

> "Judges ought to remember that their office is *jus dicere*, and not *jus dare*: to interpret law, and not to make law or give law. Else will it be like the authority claimed by the Church of Rome . . .".[15]

So the theory in England, at least from Tudor times, was that judges had to find their authority in the text of the law, just as the new Bishops were expected to find theirs in the text of Holy Scripture. It was a very English, indeed Protestant, virtue to demand fidelity to the text so as to curb the inventions and pretensions to unwarranted power. In the Church, authority had led to excessive, even absurd, claims of power, immunities, indulgences and luxuries. Churchmen had lost their connection with the ultimate source of their authority, the Bible. Even in our present age, we can see resonances of this adherence to religious texts (but also of divisions about their meaning) in current controversies in the Christian Church over women bishops, homosexual priests and so called "gay marriage".

The books of the Christian Bible were complete and known by Mediaeval times.[16] Even as Bacon was writing, they were being translated into the peerless Geneva and King James revisions. The common law, however, was not so confined. Daily it was being expanded by judges who "declared" the law, construing written instruments and, in ever greater number as the years passed, interpreting and applying statutes. In the United States of America, judges after 1789 began to construe and apply the ambiguous language of the written Constitution. Yet for all this, by the nineteenth century the "oracular view of the judicial function" took hold of most of the English judges. This was important for England's colonies (and also in the United States) because it was at this time that the notion of an international common law first began to form. Throughout the British Empire, the common law was reinforced by the decisions of the Privy Council. Generally speaking the Privy Council was, or became, a comparatively light burden for the colonies because, normally, it spoke in the language of rationality, order and freedom and commonly upheld individual rights.

Early in the nineteenth century, Baron Parke in *Mirehouse v Rennell*[17] explained the confined notion of the scope of the

---

[15] F.Bacon, "Of Judicature" in *Essays Civil and Moral*.
[16] I leave aside the plates given to Joseph Smith of the Mormons and the Dead Sea Scrolls discovered more recently.
[17] (1833) 1 Cl. & F. 527 at 546; 6 E.R. 1015 at 1023.

judicial power to reformulate old precedents where doing so would question the law as established in earlier times:

> "... We are not at liberty to reject [these rules], and to abandon all analogy to them, in those to which they have not yet been judicially applied, because we think that the rules are not as convenient and reasonable as we ourselves could have devised.

By century's end, Lord Esher M.R. in *Willis v Baddeley*[18] felt no hesitation in saying:

> "This is not a case, as has been suggested, of what is sometimes called judge-made law. There is, in fact, no such thing as judge-made law, for the judges do not make the law, though they frequently have to apply existing law to circumstances as to which it has not previously been authoritatively laid down that such law is applicable".[19]

With the growth of parliamentary legislation, this declaratory view of the judicial function was reinforced by the legal positivism of Bentham, Dicey and Austin. Law was to be found in rules. Rules appeared in written constitutions, statutes and the reasons of judges of the higher courts. Judges declared what the law required. Their function was basically one of verbal analysis and application. Such was the preferred view of most common law judges of England and its colonies well into the second half of the twentieth century. Whenever tempted to depart from the words of the past, they would usually pull themselves back to the "noble lie".[20] They would do so in the belief that any acknowledgment that they enjoyed a substantial role in expressing the law and applying it in new ways would defy the accepted political theory. It would upset other lawmakers. It would needlessly disturb the Common people who were deemed to be reassured by thinking of judges as applicators not creators: with functions *dicere* not *dare*.

STRICT AND COMPLETE LEGALISM

It sometimes happens that distance from the heart of a great empire makes those far away more extreme in their imperial

---

[18] [1892] 2 Q.B. 324.
[19] *ibid.*, at 326, with the agreement of Bowen L.J. and A. L. Smith L.J. These cases are cited in McHugh, *op. cit.*, n. 11 above, at p. 25.
[20] Lord Radcliffe, *Not in Feather Beds* (Quality Book Club, London, 1968), p. xvi.

ideology: keener than those at its seat to cling to its orthodoxy. Long after the reminder of Queen Victoria's birthday had passed into history in the United Kingdom, Empire Day was celebrated in Australia every May 24. In my schooldays, it was a time of speeches and fireworks. The politicians and judges of the United Kingdom never had the fascination for their global domain that was felt by their faithful copiers in the British realms and territories beyond the seas.

The clearest proof of this may be seen in the British rejection, after the Second World War, of the proposals for a Privy Council comprised of a full complement of Commonwealth judges, participating on equal terms.[21] The comparative neglect of Commonwealth jurisprudence in the United Kingdom until recent years was another sign. By the time these things were ready to change, the Privy Council's heyday as an imperial court had passed. A great chance was lost forever, although new and different links have since been forged.

In countries like Australia, the lawyers who occupied the highest positions in the judiciary had imbibed and accepted their legal doctrine from the Lord Eshers in London. According to their doctrine, judges did not make the law. This would certainly have been the view accepted a century ago by the foundation Justices of the High Court of Australia. Long after doubting voices had begun to whisper, then to speak and then to cry out the truth about the judicial method in Britain and the United States, the leading judges of Australia (more Catholic than the Pope) continued to proclaim the doctrinal impermissibility of judge-made innovation.

Well into the twentieth century, the creative imagination of Australia's judges was dampened by a number of factors. These included the received doctrine about the judicial role, the superintendence of Australian judicial decisions by the Privy Council and the literalist approach to statutory construction then in vogue. In other countries of the Empire, the manifest unsuitability of some rules of the common law for the differing social, economic and religious circumstances of those colonies, forced a measure of judicial creativity on the part of some colonial judges.[22] But in settler countries the judiciary, and most of the populous, wanted nothing more than to be seen as white British people, living in a civilised way under British justice although encircled by lesser breeds beyond the laws of England.

---

[21] M.Davies, "The Future of the Common Law: The Threat from Europe" (2003) 12:1 *Commonwealth Lawyer* 35, p. 37.

[22] M.D.Kirby, "Challenges to Justice in a Plural Society" (2002) 11:2 *Commonwealth Lawyer* 35. Referring to legal adaptation in colonial Malaya.

As late at 1978, a question concerning this use of imported English law arose before the High Court of Australia. The Court held that a convicted capital felon, Darcy Dugan, could not sue a newspaper for defamation because of the ancient English law of attainder and corruption of the blood.[23] The Australian judges of that time scoffed at the argument that these doctrines had not been received into the New South Wales colony at the time of British settlement.[24] It was submitted for Mr Dugan that, when Australia was settled, there were so many felons in the Australian colonies, convicted of capital and non-capital crimes but spared execution, that to deprive them all of civil rights was such an affront to the rule of law that it made the adoption of the old English law of attainder unsuitable to Australian conditions.[25] That submission was rejected by the High Court. Justice Lionel Murphy alone dissented.

Specifically, in *Dugan*, the majority poured scorn on the argument that attainder was "inappropriate . . . to more recent times",[26] or "out of harmony with modern notions".[27] Justifying the decision to apply the rule in the late twentieth century, and to withdraw from Mr Dugan the protection of the civil law of defamation, Justice Gibbs declared that an appeal to a more "appropriate law" would lead to "dangerous uncertainty as to matters of fundamental principle".[28] For his part, Justice Murphy dismissed this "static" view of the common law.[29] He said: "Judges have created the doctrine of civil death and judges can abolish it. Judges have closed the doors of the courts and judges can re-open them".

Not long after the decision in *Dugan*, the Australian Court, for similar reasons (including deference to the primary role of the legislature in changing the law[30]) declined to reconsider the law about the immunity from negligence of owners of animals straying onto adjacent highways. In 1947 in *Searle v Wallbank*,[31] the House of Lords had upheld that immunity as part of the common law of England. The Australian court simply applied the same law. Arguments addressed to suggested differences

---

[23] *Dugan v Mirror Newspapers Ltd* (1978) 142 C.L.R. 583.
[24] Blackstone, *op. cit.*, n. 12 above, p. 107.
[25] cf. *R. v Farrell, Dingle & Hoodward* (1831) 1 Legge. 5, *per* Forbes C.J (diss.), at 34.
[26] *Dugan, op. cit.*, n. 23 above, *per* Barwick C.J., p. 586.
[27] *ibid., per* Gibbs J., p. 592.
[28] *ibid.*
[29] *ibid., per* Murphy J., 611.
[30] *State Government Insurance Commission v Trigwell* (1979) 142 C.L.R. 617. Compare the more recent decision in *Brodie v Singleton Shire Council* (2001) 206 CLR 512 as to the result, methodology and reasoning of the Court.
[31] [1947] A.C. 341.

between the social, economic and highway conditions of England that had given birth to the rule and those of Australia fell on deaf judicial ears.[32] Again, only Justice Murphy dissented.

These decisions were criticised at the time by scholars who said that they represented an unnecessary abdication of the judicial role in "declaring" the common law of Australia. But nothing much changed in Australia until the mid 1980s. In part, the resistance to change reflected the personalities and opinions of the judges. In part, the Australian restraint may have been because, until 1986, most Australian judges were still looking over their shoulder to the Privy Council in London.[33] As it happens, I presided in 1986 in the Court of Appeal of New South Wales in the last Australian judgment to come under their Lordships' benign scrutiny. Happily I passed muster.

In part, the Australian restraint of the 1980s may also have arisen because the stimulus of notions of fundamental human rights did not begin to have much of a role in Australian courts until the 1990s.[34] But over and above these causes was one potent influence, which stood out. It was the impact on the Australian legal psyche of a doctrinal position adopted by Sir Owen Dixon. Dixon had served as a Justice of the High Court of Australia from 1929, and as Chief Justice for twelve years after 1952. By the power of his legal knowledge, the reputation of his judgments and the effectiveness of the exposition of his philosophy in and out of court, he taught generations of Australian judges, lawyers, law teachers and students that "there is no other safe guide to judicial decisions in great conflicts than a strict and complete legalism."[35]

Dixon confidently and proudly remarked that the court over which he presided was, by some, "thought to be excessively legalistic". He declared that he would be "sorry to think that it is anything else".[36] Although these words were written with specific reference to the resolution of federal conflicts under the Australian Constitution (where, as Dixon observed, there was a

[32] *Trigwell, op. cit.*, n. 30 above, *per* Gibbs J., at 627–628; *per* Mason J., at 634–635 (with whom Barwick C.J., Stephen and Aickin J.J. agreed).

[33] Appeals to the Privy Council from Australian courts were successively abolished by Privy Council (Limitation of Appeals) Act 1968 (Cth); Privy Council (Appeals from the High Court) Act 1975 (Cth) and Australia Act 1986 (UK and Cth), s. 11(1). See *Kirmani v Captain Cook Cruises Pty Ltd [No 2]; Ex parte Attorney-General (Qld)* (1985) 159 C.L.R. 461, *per* Gibbs C.J., Mason, Wilson, Brennan, Deane and Dawson J.J., at 464–465.

[34] Most especially in *Mabo v Queensland [No 2]* (1992) 175 C.L.R. 1 and *Minister for Immigration and Ethnic Affairs v Teoh* (1995) 183 C.L.R. 273.

[35] *Swearing in of Sir Owen Dixon as Chief Justice* (1952) 85 C.L.R. xi at p. xiv.

[36] *ibid.*

special need for the courts to "maintain the confidence of all parties") there is no doubt that this was Dixon's general approach to judging. It was an approach that he deployed with great effect over nearly half of the life of the High Court of Australia.

Long after he was gone, and even today, the power of Dixon's exposition and example continue to influence the notion of what it is to be a judge in Australia. His words provide a powerful rallying cry for those within the law of a conservative disposition. Those who do not agree with Dixon's exposition of legalism, and who suggest that, in its day, it was honoured as much in the breach as in the observance, are commonly denounced as judicial activists. Yet, as I shall show, the fault line that has appeared in this debate can also be found far from Australia.

Dixon's views—and like opinions of exponents of the same doctrine—became an ideology. They provided a banner under which now march a motley band of followers. Some of today's "strict legalists" are merely nostalgic, like those who pine for the return of a faded empire. Some are fine jurists searching for a meaning to the law that is larger and more objective than their own perceived frailties. But some are politicians of differing stripes who know nothing of the common law and its marvellous creativity, are contemptuous of fundamental human rights and jealous of any source of lawmaking power apart from their own. Some are the spokesmen of powerful interests who hate it when judges express the law in terms of legal principles to protect minorities, the weak and the vulnerable.

This, then, is the debate that is the subject of these lectures. It is a debate vital for the proper boundaries of the judicial function. My thesis is that a return in the twenty-first century to a world in which "judges do not make the law", a world that is proudly "excessively legalistic", a world of "strict and complete legalism" is neither possible nor desirable. That place is the world of *Brigadoon*—a place of smoke and mists that never really existed as portrayed, except in metaphor and imagination. If we could re-create it now, it would be a cruel place of indifference to the fact that judges have choices, that such choices are inherent in the common law system itself and that, giving a meaning to uncertain words and phrases, rules and principles is the daily work that judges actually do.

To return to Dixon's "excessive legalism" would be to take a journey back into a world of deception, where judges pretended to a mechanical function whilst knowing, when they stop to think about it, that they play a vital role in *making law*. Today there is room for legitimate differences over the occasions and scope of creativity proper to judges of our legal tradition. But a return to "strict and complete legalism" of the judge-as-mechanic is not the way to go. Judges and lawyers of the common law need to engage intellectually with this issue. Unless they do so, the gains of the legal Reformation of the past twenty years could be lost. The honesty and transparency that has come with those gains could be buried as the present Counter-Reformation gains momentum in a determined endeavour of an influential minority to restore "the former condition of things".[37]

If any judge or lawyer in the United Kingdom feels safe, in the current enlightenment, from a return to the "noble lie" that judges merely apply the law, they need only reflect on the comparative brevity of that enlightenment, the determination of the forces now aligned against it and the course which the debate on judicial activism has lately taken in other countries. In these lectures I will describe what is happening. With the global common law come global movements, both for good and ill. As the United Kingdom moves towards the creation of its own Supreme Court[38]—even one very different from that of the United States and Australia[39]—it is as well to be alert to the controversies that tend to beset such courts. The visibility, mode of appointment, functions and public role of the judges of such courts tend to make them and their institutions a lightning rod for those who resent their power and who challenge their decisions, particularly where those decisions affirm the rights of the weak against the powerful.

These lectures, then, represent a morality tale told by an Australian child of the common law at a moment in the history of the law in the United Kingdom when great change is in the air. The least that such a child can do, having come to maturity, is to share with the parent warnings of things afoot elsewhere in a dangerous world.

But first I must tell the story of the judicial Reformation that preceded the current times. It is a happy tale, as most stories of honesty, candour and the search for justice in the world of law

---

[37] J.D.Heydon, "Judicial Activism and the Death of the Rule of Law" (2003) 23:2 *Australian Bar Review* 110, p. 133. The speech was originally published in *Quadrant* (Jan/Feb 2003; vol. XLVII, No. 1), 9. References are to the *Australian Bar Review* version.

[38] United Kingdom, Department for Constitutional Affairs, *Constitutional Reform: A Supreme Court for the United Kingdom*, Consultation Paper, Cmnd. 11/03 (2003).

[39] *ibid.*, at pp. 8 and 21.

tend to be. Those who hanker for a return to the fairytale, and the restoration of the former condition of things, must first be made to listen to the enlightenment that came over the common law in most of its branches as the twentieth century drew to its close. It is an enlightenment which the Counter-Reformation seeks to put into reverse.

2. Reformation

INHERENT IN THE THING

My first lecture concerned the Old Testament of "strict and complete legalism".[40] The view that judges make no law; they only apply it. Now I will describe the legal Reformation—a period of enlightenment, candour and transparency. The legal Reformation was gradually embraced by judges and other lawyers of many lands. It gained urgency as the twentieth century drew to its close. My description of the change will provide a springboard for my later examination of contemporary attempts to launch a Counter-Reformation: demonising judicial honesty and integrity as "judicial activism" in the hope of restoring the old doctrine and methodology: an endeavour that should be resisted.[41]

Looking back, our eyes are now released from the blinkers of the judicial orthodoxy of earlier times. We can see how unrealistic the dogma of "strict and complete legalism" in the judicial method really was. Contemporary defenders of the old notions accept that occasional doctrinal advances in the common law were legitimate, so long as such changes "grew" strictly out of past precedents; were derived solely by a vague and self-fulfilling methodology of "strict logic and high technique"[42] and ignored policy, especially social policy[43] inherent in considering alternative decisions. Even allowing for such concessions to reality, the doctrine is still deceitful. It was not, in fact, "rooted

---

[40] Dixon, *op. cit.*, n. 35 above, at p. xiv.

[41] R.Sackville, "Why Do Judges Make Law? Some Aspects of Judicial Law Making" (2001) 5 *University Western Sydney Law Review* 59 at p. 63; cf. W. W. Justice, "Two Faces of Judicial Activism", *Judges on Judging—Views from the Bench* (D. M. O'Brien ed., Chatham House, Chatham, 1997) 302, p. 302.

[42] F.W.Maitland, Introduction, *Selden Society Year Book Series*, vol. 1 at p. xviii, cited Heydon, *op. cit.*, n. 37 above, at p. 5.

[43] *Rootes v Shelton* (1967) 116 C.L.R. 383, *per* Kitto J., at 386–387 reversing *Rootes v Shelton* [1966] 2 N.S.W.R. 784.

in the Inns of Court, rooted in the *Year Books*, rooted in the centuries", to use Maitland's poetic metaphors. On the contrary, it was rooted in deception: deception of the community, of other lawmakers and, perhaps most worrying of all, of the judiciary and legal profession itself.

The law of England, which the countries of the British Empire received in various forms, has been in a process of development and evolution over nearly eight hundred years.[44] On this journey, the common law has adapted itself to many companions: the Royal prerogative, the emerging principles of equity, the growing body of statute law and, recently, the imperatives of constitutional texts and human rights instruments. The interaction of these sources, in millions of judicial decisions, has stimulated a body of law that reflects individual judicial attempts to produce outcomes that conformed to rules and secured results that appeared lawful, just and appropriate in the conditions in which the decisions were made. We should not be ashamed of this extraordinary creation. On the contrary, it is a marvellous tale: combining continuity and flexibility, predicability and change.

The song of the common law has been sung by singers of differing talents and aspirations. Because the song was originally an English one, it contains many maritime references. Lord Wright described judicial creativity by reference to judicial mariners: clinging to the coast of settled rules to which they must repeatedly return for safety and reassurance.[45] Justice Kitto, in Australia, denounced a wholly reasonable attempt by Justice Jacobs (later himself a member of the High Court of Australia) to test a suggested principle of the common law by reference to judicial policy. Kitto administered a watery reproof:

> "If I may be pardoned for saying so, to discuss [a] case in terms of 'judicial policy' and 'social expediency' is to introduce deleterious foreign matter into the waters of the common law—in which, after all, we have no more than riparian rights".[46]

But it was probably Judge Learned Hand, in the United States, who found the most accurate aquatic simile:

> "The whole structure of the common law . . . stands as a monument slowly raised, like a coral reef, from the minute accretions of past

---

[44] A.F.Mason, "The Judge as Law-Maker" (1996) 3 *James Cook University L. Rev.* 1, p. 5.
[45] Lord Wright, "The Study of Law" (1938) 54 L.Q.R. 185, p. 186.
[46] *Rootes* (HCA), *op. cit.*, n. 43 above, at 386–387.

individuals of whom each built upon the relics which his predecessors left and in turn left a foundation upon which his successors might work".[47]

Any attempt to stamp on such a semi-chaotic, intermittent creation, a scientific dogma of "strict and complete legalism" fashioned by pure logic and so-called "high technique" was, frankly, absurd. Logic alone and reason isolated from everything else could not decide new cases. The path of the common law, and the methodology of its judges, have not been fashioned by logic alone; but by experience, as Justice Holmes in the United States famously observed.[48] The common law is a product of judgment and opinion—created over the centuries by people used to wielding such powers.

It was the United States jurists of the twentieth century, rather than common law writers of the British Empire and Commonwealth, who first challenged head-on the declaratory theory of the judicial function and the strict formalism of the English legal positivists. In doing so, the American jurists were not describing things unique to the United States, with its admittedly different constitutional system and judicial tradition. They were looking deep into the very "structure of the common law".[49] Unsurprisingly, when they looked there, and into their own daily experience, they found a much greater element of judicial creativity than was publicly admitted. Indeed, judicial creativity lay deeply embedded in the very nature of the common law as they practised it.

Being made up of a myriad of decisions, the common law encouraged its practitioners to search for the perfect precedent: one exactly "on point". In England until well into the twentieth century, legal education was not normally carried out in the universities but in the Inns of Court. Typically, the teachers were not scholars. They were experienced judges and practising lawyers. This feature of instruction in the craft of law was imitated in many parts of the world. The problem inherent in this method of deriving and describing legal rules, was its tendency towards procedural and substantive rigidity: legal outcomes depending heavily on the degree of insight of those who decided earlier cases and those who taught them. To gain release from rigid outcomes it was commonly thought necessary

[47] B.Learned Hand, Review (1922) 35 *Harvard Law Review*, 479, p. 479.
[48] O.W.Holmes Jr., *The Common Law* (1881) (Mark De Wolfe Howe ed., Macmillan, London, 1968), p. 1.
[49] Learned Hand, *op. cit.*, n. 47 above, at p. 479.

to resort to equity[50] or to an appeal to a new rule of the common law derived from its pursuit of the "perfection of [human] reason".[51]

The attempt of Lord Chief Justice Coke to isolate a notion of "the reason of natural law" as the ultimate source of all legal obligations (and to elevate it to a power exceeding even that of the King[52]) has modern supporters.[53] In countries, like my own, which accept a written constitution as the ultimate legal *Grundnorm*,[54] it is a notion that does not fit well with legal theory or political reality. However, the development of the common law as a more coherent source of rules was undoubtedly stimulated by the attempts of great judges, such as Coke, Maitland and their successors to re-express a "rule", fashioned for a given case, into a rule broader than perhaps was necessary to decide the instant case. In this way those great judges sought to stamp on the chaos of past decisional authority a retrospective doctrinal order that the makers of that past authority may not themselves have imagined.[55] The work of such judges was picked up and carried forward by law teachers and text writers, striving to reduce the chaos of individual decisions to the form of emerging principles which they collected, classified and described.

Blackstone's *Commentaries on the Laws of England* fashioned old precedents into many new legal categories and concepts. Those *Commentaries* proved most influential, especially in the United States, cut off as it was after the revolution from its original source in England. Yet the general principles of the common law that emerged in the nineteenth century were often the product of highly selective case citations by judges and textwriters.[56] It

---

[50] M.H.McHugh, "The Judicial Method" (1999) 73 *Australian Law Journal* 37 at p. 44 referring to *Cowcher v Cowcher* [1972] 1 W.L.R. 425 at 430.

[51] Sir Edward Coke, *Institute of the Lawes of England* (1628), p. 97b as quoted in Parkinson, *op. cit.*, n. 13 above, p. 179; D F Forte, *Natural Law and Contemporary Public Policy* (Georgetown University Press, 1998), p. 4.

[52] F.Bennion, "Nature of Legal Policy" in *Statutory Interpretation* (4th ed., Butterworths, London, 2002) p. 657, p. 696 referring to *Dr Bonham's Case*, (1610) 8 Co. Rep. 107a at 118a; 77 E.R. 638 at 652.

[53] *e.g. Taylor v New Zealand Poultry Board* [1984] 1 N.Z.L.R. 394, *per* Cooke J., at 398; *Fraser v State Services Commission* [1984] 1 N.Z.L.R. 116, *per* Cooke J., at 121; *New Zealand Drivers' Association v New Zealand Road Carriers* [1982] 1 N.Z.L.R. 374 *per* Cooke P., McMullin and Ongley J.J., at 390. See generally M D Kirby, "Lord Cooke and Fundamental Rights" in *The Struggle for Simplicity in the Law—Essays for Lord Cooke of Thorndon* (P Rishworth ed., Butterworths, Wellington, 1997) 331, p. 345–346.

[54] *Durham Holdings Pty Ltd v New South Wales* (2001) 205 C.L.R. 399, *per* Gaudron, McHugh, Gummow and Hayne J.J., at 410; *per* Kirby J., at 422.

[55] Parkinson, *op. cit.*, n. 13, above, p. 180.

[56] *ibid.*, p. 181.

was this judicial and textual selectivity that created the modern common law rather than "strict logic and high technique". Judges were usually so busy deciding cases that the substantial re-conceptualisation and development of legal principle had to be left to later and to others.

INSTITUTIONAL REINFORCEMENT

Certain institutional features of the common law tended to increase, rather than to diminish, judicial creativity. Those institutional considerations help to explain the tendency of the common law to grow and develop in a pragmatic rather than a strictly logical way.

First, must be mentioned the manner of the selection of the senior judiciary. This was important because it was to those judges that the development of the common law, the invention of the principles of equity and the interpretation of statutes and exposition of written constitutions was chiefly entrusted.

Almost without exception, these judges came from a comparatively small group of lawyers. Before judicial appointment, they were normally socialised in a cohesive Bar. They generally shared a common socio-economic background. At the Bar they were typically organised along hierarchical lines. They usually exhibited a high degree of homogeneity of outlook and attitude about legal outcomes. Such features of the key players were reinforced by the humdrum activities of daily practice together.[57] Such considerations, operating for the most part in a comparatively stable social and legal setting, tended to encourage a self-image of political sterilisation of the judiciary as a class.

Within this class, the judiciary confidently evolved the rules of common law and equity by reference to broadly shared notions of public interest and legal policy.[58] It was inevitable that they would do so. They did not need to spell out their methodology. Self confidence and resolute action in terms of shared values were the hallmarks of the judges of the common law tradition.

To this day, European legal scholars, looking at the judiciary of our system, regard creativity not only as inevitable but as a

---

[57] cf. C.Guarnieri and P.Pederzoli, *The Power of Judges—A Comparative Study of Courts and Democracy* (English ed. C. A. Thomas) (O.U.P., Oxford, 2002), p. 70. The homogeneity was acknowledged by Lord Devlin as a relevant factor: P. Devlin, "Judges, Government and Politics" (1978) 41 *Modern Law Review* 501, p. 505.

[58] cf. *Fender v St John Mildenay* [1938] A.C. 1, *per* Lord Wright, at 38; Bennion, *op. cit.*, n. 52 above, p. 671.

saving grace of the common law technique. They portray the judiciary of the common law as resorting to legal inventions whenever the law was brought face to face with serious ambiguities, uncertainties and anomalies that needed to be adapted to contemporary social aspirations.[59] When the homogeneity and shared attitudes of the past came under challenge, new sources of legal principle were devised to take their place. The ease with which this may be done is usually a source of admiration and envy on the part of those who work within different legal systems, with less opportunity for creative adaptation.

Secondly, the judicial obligation to give reasons is important in this context.[60] That duty discourages a naked usurpation of power by judges.[61] Yet, in responding to the arguments of the parties, a judge must engage, in published reasons, in a kind of dialogue between the past and the present; between the rules in the books and the unique circumstances of the particular case. As judges of the legal Reformation in the late twentieth century felt themselves released from the straight-jacket of "excessive legalism", they became more willing to expose, and to discuss frankly, the considerations of principle and policy that were affecting their minds as they worked towards their decisions. Once encouraged to explain their reasoning in this transparent way, it became very difficult to return the judicial dialogue to the sterile pretence that solutions for all legal problems are to be found in the language or logic of a past decision or the unambiguous text of a statute or a written constitution, with nothing else required. When the genie of full and truthful reasons escaped, it became hard to persuade the law's practitioners to return to the old deceit of formalism.

Thirdly, the right of judges in collegiate courts to dissent, and to express a differing opinion is another feature of the common law system that reinforces judicial creativity. The very diversity of judicial opinions about the outcome of a particular case represents a reminder of the indeterminate nature of much judicial decision-making. As we all know, today's dissent occasionally becomes tomorrow's orthodoxy.

[59] Guarnieri and Pederzoli, *op. cit.*, n. 57 above, p. 70; cf. M. Lasser, "Do Judges Deploy Policy?" (2001) 22 *Cardozo L. Rev.* 863 at p. 887 citing D. Kennedy, *A Critique of Adjudication: Fin de Siecle* (Harvard University Press, Boston, 1997), p. 108.

[60] In Australia this has been upheld as a universal feature of the administration of justice in the courts: *Public Service Board of NSW v Osmond* (1986) 159 C.L.R. 656, *per* Gibbs C.J., at 666. Contrast the position under civil law: *Lasser, op. cit.*, n. 59 above, at p. 898.

[61] Parkinson, *op. cit.*, n. 13 above, p. 195.

In most civil law countries, judges are obliged to disguise their disagreements in vagaries of ambiguous language or to swallow their differences in institutionally imposed silence. This has not been the way of the common law. The publicly revealed diversity of our reasons affirms the fact that highly trained professional judges of ability and undoubted integrity, applying their notions of what the law is, quite often came to strikingly differing results. Commonly, these outcomes are influenced by different perceptions of the facts; by disagreement over the applicable legal authority; or by disputes over what the judges see as the relevant theory, principle or values at stake in the decision.

So far as "logic and high technique" are concerned, Lord Buckmaster's dissent in *Donoghue v Stevenson*[62] was as much an arguable development from the precedents of past decisions on the law of negligence as was Lord Atkin's famous reformulation. Lord Atkin set out to show that the earlier cases on negligence could be explained by reference to an emerging and over-arching general theory. Lord Buckmaster contested this conclusion. Yet it was Lord Atkin's bold approach that eventually gained acceptance.[63] The sharp differences and frequent contradictions of judicial reasoning in the common law tradition, illustrate the intellectual emptiness of "pure" legalism. Through dissenting opinions, whether we agree or disagree with them, we frequently come to understand how others, without the slightest incompetence, dishonesty or legal heresy, can reach opposite conclusions. Often those conclusions are influenced by expressed or unexpressed divergences over the legal authority, principles or policy applicable to the case.

Fourthly, the existence of the jury was another institutional reminder of the limits which the common law (like so many other features of English government), placed upon pure theory and strict logic. The fact that, when penalties were most severe and decisions were most important, the final arbiter of contested facts was often not a professional judge but citizen jurors, reinforced the limits which the legal system placed on carrying logic to extremes.[64] Many a convict who later founded a distinguished family in Australia would have been hanged in England if the common law and its officer-holders had been unbending devotees of strict logic.[65] The judge, sworn to apply

---

[62] *op. cit.*, n. 9 above, *per* Lord Buckmaster, at 567; *per* Lord Atkin, at 580.

[63] McHugh, *op. cit.*, n. 50 above, at p. 44; cf. *Robinson v Tait* [2002] 2 N.Z.L.R. 30, *per* Thomas J., at 37.

[64] Bennion, *op. cit.*, n. 52 above, p. 667.

[65] *Mackenzie v The Queen* (1997) 190 C.L.R. 348, *per* Gaudron, Gummow and Kirby J.J., at 367.

the law, was a member of a culture traditionally, and rightly, suspicious of logical extremes and the techniques of reasoning that produced them. The tempering influence of principle and policy was crucial to the development of the common law.

Fifthly, in the hands of a comparatively powerful judiciary, confident and small in number, the common law frequently assumed a beneficial role as a guardian of the fundamental rights of the people.[66] A *cadre* of strong and creative individuals could play a large part in the process of legal renewal. They could do so simply because of the offices they held in a centralised, hierarchical judiciary whose orders were obeyed by those affected. Their influence was enhanced, in turn, by the power of their ideas and the felt needs of the times.

Lord Denning, with his usual modesty, likened his own efforts to re-express the principles of the common law and of equity to the earlier, similar endeavours of Lord Mansfield.[67] In Australia, the Justices of the High Court in the 1990s played an equally creative role during the decade in which Chief Justices Mason and Brennan presided over the Court. It was a time when many unsatisfactory legal rules of the past were re-examined by the Court, found to be wanting and re-expressed[68] or abolished.[69] As not uncommonly happens, after such an interval, there is now a period of absorption and even some reversal of such changes. This is further evidence of the common law system's search for a middle way. Yet a pause does not mean that the advance was wrong when it happened. Nor does it imply that it is either desirable or possible for the "former condition of things . . . to be restored", as if nothing has occurred.

PUBLIC POLICY

From the foregoing it might be imagined that it took the American realists, such as Pound, Holmes, Cardozo, Learned

---

[66] Guarnieri and Pederzoli, *op. cit.*, n. 57 above, p. 96.

[67] In *What Next in the Law* (Butterworths, London, 1982). See Bennion, *op. cit.*, n. 51 above, pp. 683–684. In decisions of cases in tort liability, Lord Denning placed emphasis on identifying the relevant public policy in new duty situations: *Spartan Steel and Alloys Ltd v Martin and Co* [1973] Q.B. 27; *Dutton v Bognor Regis UDS* [1972] 1 Q.B. 373.

[68] Some of the cases are collected in M. D. Kirby, "Courts and Policy: The Exciting Australian Scene" (1993) 19 *Commonwealth Law Bulletin* 1794 at pp. 1802–1807; McHugh, *op. cit.*, n. 50 above, at pp. 45–46.

[69] As in *The Queen v L* (1991) 174 C.L.R. 379 (marital rape) and *Mabo, op. cit.*, n. 34 above (native title to land).

Hand, Karl Llewellyn and others to shake common law from its illusions and to bring that law into contact with the reality of judicial policy choices. It is not to diminish the powerful influence of the American writers to point out that, in at least one area of the common law, the doctrine of public policy, English judges of the nineteenth century, and their successors everywhere, were engaged in debates over judicial policy that have become still broader and noisier in recent times.

The common law doctrine of public policy has been traced to the *Year Books* in 1413[70] and to the writings of Littleton and Coke. In the nineteenth century, after the impetus of Lord Mansfield, public policy came to be used as a check on the pursuit of contractual or tortious remedies that were deemed "injurious to members of the public", "against the public benefit" or "repugnant to the interests of the State".[71] To the extent that the notion of public policy was invoked by judges, it was treated as deeply ingrained in the very nature of the common law. By one of its exponents it was seen as existing for the dominant purpose of upholding the good of the community as the supreme law of the land.[72]

Justice Holmes, in a famous passage, included "intuitions of public policy" amongst the motive forces of the common law. He included these with "the felt necessities of the times, the prevalence of moral and political theories . . . even the prejudices which judges share with their fellow man".[73] Holmes declared that such forces had "a good deal more to do with the syllogisms of determining the rules by which men should be governed" than was usually admitted. Left at this level of generality, the invocation of "public policy" might be thought of as a useful, and generally negative, restraint on the application of a legal rule to circumstances beyond the point where the rule was intended to operate. However, the immediate difficulty of such a rule of "public policy" was that minds could easily differ over the contents of such policy. What should judges then do? Would pre-existing law, or strict logic, resolve the difference of opinion over a new case?

In 1826 in *Fletcher v Sondes*,[74] the rule of illegality in contracts was said to mean "that doctrine cannot be law which injures the

---

[70] Knight, *op. cit.*, n. 13 above, at p. 207.

[71] Cited *ibid.*, at p. 209.

[72] *ibid.*, at pp. 208–209 referring to such cases as *Rex v Waddington* (1800) 1 East. 143; 102 E.R. 56.

[73] *op. cit.*, n. 48 above, p. 1. Discussed T. I. Lowi, "Policy at the Intersection of Law and Politics" unpublished keynote speech, 2 Symposium, Fall 2002 in *Cornell Journal of Law and Public Policy* (forthcoming).

[74] (1826) 3 Bing. 501, *per* Best C.J., at 590; 130 E.R. 606 at 641. See also Knight, *op. cit.*, n. 13 above, at p. 209.

rights of individuals and will be productive of evil to the Church and to the community". Nowadays, the reference to "evil to the Church" strikes a somewhat discordant, even irrelevant, note. Times change. An unthinking application of that precedent today, in contemporary secular communities whether in Britain or Australia, would be regarded as absurd. "Strict logic and high technique" would not be adequate to derive a modern rule from such a ruling.

The recognition of the difficulty of defining, or even describing, the content of "public policy" led to one of the major judicial controversies of nineteenth century England. In one case in 1874, the Privy Council described it as "the *so-called* policy of the law" and "the *supposed* policy of the law". By these descriptions their Lordships disclosed their scepticism about the utility, or even existence, of such a legal doctrine.[75]

Judges who were dubious about their capacity to discern the contents of "public policy", and doubtful that it represented something that should be taken into account in legal decision-making, commonly regarded public policy as a "very unruly horse and when once astride it you never know where it will carry you".[76] This equine metaphor must be one of the most quoted in the lawbooks.[77] Yet the way judges so often return to it illustrates the extent to which the supposed principles of public policy have continued to trouble common law courts. Originally, the "unruly horse" appeared in a passage where the judge describing it felt obliged to "protest . . . against arguing too strongly upon public policy". He declared that, doing so, "may lead you from the sound law. It is never argued at all", he remarked, "but when other points fail".[78]

Despite these weaknesses in the common law doctrine of public policy, in certain corners of the law it has been applied to concrete circumstances in ways that the judges invoking it have felt to be useful, indeed essential, for the attainment of a lawful

---

[75] *Evanturel v Evanturel* (1874) L.R. 6 P.C. 1, *per curiam*, at 29 noted Knight, *ibid.*, at 213.
[76] *Richardson v Mellish* (1824) 2 Bing 229, *per* Burrough J., at 252; 130 E.R. 294 at 303.
[77] See *e.g. Foster v Driscoll* [1929] 1 K.B. 470 at 498; *Nelson v Nelson* (1995) 184 C.L.R. 538, *per* Toohey J., at 541; *New Jersey v Reading Co* 451 U.S. 918, *per* Rehnquist J. (diss.), at 919 (1980); *Barns v Barns* (2003) 77 A.L.J.R. 734, *per* Kirby J., at 757; 196 A.L.R. 65, at 98.
[78] *Richardson, op. cit.*, n. 76 above, 2 Bing 229, *per* Burrough J., at 252; 180 E.R. 294 at 303.

and just outcome in the case.[79] Why, then, did the judges invoke "public policy" in such a wide variety of circumstances over such a long period of time?

In his Hamlyn Lectures Patrick Atiyah saw the doctrine of "public policy" as an instance of the hostility of the common law towards pure theory. For him, it revealed a deep inclination of the common law towards pragmatism.[80] Other writers have suggested that the essential purpose of the doctrine was to bring broader social interests affecting the public at large into judicial consideration, so as to harmonise the pursuit of individual rights with the needs of the entire community for whose interests the judge was viewed as guardian.[81]

Clearly, the very flexibility of the content of "public policy", as relevant to the norms of the common law, has been a reason for its enduring appeal. The attempt of a Lord Chancellor in 1891 to freeze the categories of contracts that would be treated as contrary to public policy[82] failed abysmally. It failed because of the recognition, and repeated demonstration, that what is contrary, or conformable, to public policy in one era will probably be quite different soon afterwards. The reference to the "evil to the Church" in 1826, that seems so odd when read with today's eyes, is a case in point.

A few examples serve to illustrate this proposition further. They include the law's approaches to blasphemy;[83] maintenance and champerty;[84] immunity of advocates from civil liability for

---

[79] *Thornsten Nordenfeldt v Maxim Nordenfeldt Guns and Ammunition Co Ltd* [1894] A.C. 535, *per* Lord Watson, at 553; *Wilkinson v Osborne* (1915) 21 C.L.R. 89, *per* Isaacs J., at 97; *Stevens v Keogh* (1946) 72 C.L.R. 1, *per* Dixon J., at 28; *Nelson, op. cit.*, n. 77 above, *per* McHugh J., at 611.

[80] P.Atiyah, *Pragmatism and Theory in English Law* (39th Hamlyn Lectures, 1987) (Stevens, London, 1977), p. 143 *et seq.*

[81] C.R.Symmons, "The Function and Effect of Public Policy in Contemporary Common Law" (1977) 51 *Australian Law Journal* 185 at p. 189.

[82] *In re Miriams* [1891] 1 Q.B. 594, *per* Cave J., at 595, noted H. L. Friendly, "The Courts and Social Policy: Substance and Procedure" in *Judges on Judging— Views from the Bench* (D. M. O'Brien ed., Chatham House, Chatham, 1997) 289, at p. 290.

[83] *Bowman v Secular Society Ltd* [1917] A.C. 406; P. Winfield, "Public Policy in the English Common Law" (1929) 42 *Harvard Law Rev* 76 at p. 95; Bennion, *op. cit.*, n. 52 above, pp. 662–663; and S. Judd, "The Unruly Horse Put Out to Pasture: The Doctrine of Public Policy in the Modern Law of Contract" (1996) 8 *Auckland University Law Review* 686 at p. 710.

[84] *Stevens v Keogh* (1946) 72 C.L.R. 1, *per* Dixon J., at 28; *Thai Trading Co Ltd v Taylor* [1998] 3 All E.R. 65, *per* Millett L.J., at 69; Bennion, *op. cit.*, n. 52 above, p. 664.

negligence;[85] prostitution;[86] official action contrary to law;[87] standing to sue;[88] and the legal status and rights of children in relation to their parents.[89] These are just a few instances in which changes in "public policy" have been invoked to justify a change in judicial outcomes. Was this simply judicial activism—nothing more than judges responding to their own prejudices and values and making it up as they went along? Or were the judges in these cases attempting to state the law, in what were clearly new social circumstances, by the use of a broad explanatory principle, necessarily of changing content? After all, we could not continue to reason in terms of "evil to the Church". How was that to be explained by a judge deciding a later case in a very different world?

The greater willingness of contemporary judges to acknowledge the importance of changing social conditions to their decisions has only come about following the pitched battles in the nineteenth century in which adherents to different opinions about "public policy" expounded their respective views. Often they did so with a passion that seems familiar to readers of contemporary debates over judicial activism.

For every adherent to the sceptical school of wild horses, such as Mr Justice Burrough[90], there was a Lord Chief Justice Pollock who found the notion of "public policy" to be extremely useful to his judicial reasoning. In *Egerton v Brownlow*,[91] Pollock declared that, if he were to discard "public policy" from judicial consideration he would be abdicating the functions of his office. On the contrary, he said, he ought not to shrink from applying the principles of public policy to "any new and extraordinary case that may arise". He asserted that "all matters relating to the public welfare—all acts of the legislature or the Executive—must be decided and determined on their own merits". For these remarks today, in some places at least, he would doubtless be denounced as a brazen "judicial activist".

---

[85] cf. *Giannarelli v Wraith* (1988) 165 C.L.R. 543, *per* Mason J., at 555; *Boland v Yates Property Corporation* (1999) 167 A.L.R. 575, *per* Kirby J., at 611; *Arthur J. S Hall v Simons* [2000] A.C. 543.

[86] Judd, *op. cit.*, n. 83 above, at p. 688, referring to a case where a commercial sex worker sued a client for alleged breach of contract.

[87] *The Queen v Ireland* (1970) 126 C.L.R. 321, *per* Barwick C.J., at 335; *Bunning v Cross* (1978) 141 C.L.R. 54; *Ridgeway v The Queen* (1995) 184 C.L.R. 19.

[88] *Inland Revenue Commissioners v National Federation of Self Employed; R. v Treasury; Ex parte Smedley* [1985] Q.B. 657, *per* Slade L.J., at 669; Bennion, *op. cit.*, n. 52 above, pp. 662–663.

[89] *Dunlap v Dunlap* (1931) 71 *American Law Reports* 1055 noted in *Symmons, op. cit.*, n. 81 above, at p. 189.

[90] In *Richardson, op. cit.*, n. 76 above.

[91] (1853) 4 H.L. Cas. 1 at 149; 10 E.R. 359 at 419.

Reviewing these apparent departures from "strict legalism" in legal doctrine, Professor Winfield in 1929, in words that also seem fresh today, remarked of the judges who opposed the use of public policy to explain their reasoning:

> "Perhaps . . . like all English judges, they were practical men, not at all welcoming any statement of the theory of judicial legislation. When this theory peeped out from behind the veil of public policy . . . most of them were so alarmed at its appearance that they promptly hustled it back again, and seemed disposed to deny the existence not only of the theory but also of the veil which covered it. They might have pardoned an angel for having entertained it unawares, but they could not forgive it for appearing to them in nothing but its wings".[92]

The use of "public policy" in our law illustrates the limits of strict logic and the scope for judicial creativity. But what is creativity and what is restraint? This issue arose recently in the House of Lords[93] and the High Court of Australia[94] in cases concerning claims by parents of children, born after a failed sterilisation procedure, who have sued to recover the economic costs of raising their unexpected child.

In the Australian case both parties argued their respective propositions of public policy at length. The surgeon and those opposing recovery of damages by the parents cited Biblical texts;[95] the traditional common law respect for human life;[96] the supposed analogy to the restrictions on recovery of pure economic loss;[97] resistance to the alleged commodification of human life; and even the requirements of otherwise rarely cited international human rights treaties[98] to show that such recovery was contrary to law. On the other hand, the parents claiming damages relied on strict judicial adherence to the general principles of negligence recovery;[99] the burden of persuasion which, they asserted, was carried by those who sought a

---

[92] Winfield, *op. cit.*, n. 83 above, at p. 89.
[93] *Mcfarlane v Tayside Health Board* [2000] A.C. 59, *per* Lord Clyde, at 100–101. See also *Rees v Darlington Memorial Hospital NHS Trust* [2003] 3 W.L.R. 1091.
[94] *Cattanach v Melchior* (2003) 77 A.L.J.R. 1312; 199 A.L.R. 131.
[95] *St John's Gospel*, 16:21 in the Christian Bible. See *C.E.S. v SuperClinics (Aust) Pty Ltd* (1995) 38 N.S.W.L.R. 47, *per* Meagher J.A., at 87.
[96] *Cattanach, op. cit.*, n. 94 above, *per* Gleeson C.J., 77 A.L.J.R. 1312 at 1321; 199 A.L.R. 131 at 142–143.
[97] *ibid.*, *per* Gleeson C.J., 77 A.L.J.R. 1312; 199 A.L.R. 131 at 144.
[98] *ibid.*
[99] As stated in *Livingstone v Rawyards Coal Company* (1880) 5 App. Cas. 25, *per* Lord Blackburn, at 39.

departure from such principles; the general retreat of the common law from recognising zones of immunity for particular professional people;[100] and the need to redress the particular burden which such an immunity would impose on women and mothers to which earlier judicial decisions may not have been adequately attentive.[101]

Allowing for the distinction between public policy and the general policy of the law,[102] the Australian decision on failed sterilisation is notable for the candid discussion, in each of the six opinions, of the issues of public policy and legal policy which the case was seen as presenting. None of the judges in the case—not one—pretended that the decision could be discovered solely by the application of logic to past legal authority. None approached his conclusion only by a technique of "strict logic", whether described as "high", "low" or otherwise. In my reasons, I drew this feature of the case to notice because denunciation of "judicial activism" is common in Australia just now.[103] In his reasons, Justice Callinan, who favoured recovery, went even further:

> "I cannot help observing that the repeated disavowal in the cases of recourse to public policy is not always convincing . . . [I]t would be more helpful for the resolution of the controversy if judges frankly acknowledged their debt to their own social values, and the way in which they have in fact moulded or influenced their judgments rather than the application of strict legal principle".[104]

JUDICIAL CHOICE

So what has changed since the judicial agonising in the nineteenth century cases over "public policy"? What has occurred since the early twentieth century embrace of the legal theology of "strict and complete legalism"? How have contemporary judges in Australia, England and elsewhere come to invite debate about, and to participate in, candid discussion of

---

[100] *Cattanach, op. cit.,* n. 94 above, *per* Kirby J., 77 A.L.J.R. 1312 at 1348; 199 A.L.R. 131 at 180.

[101] *ibid., per* Kirby J., 77 A.L.J.R. 1312 at 1343; 199 A.L.R. 131 at 172.

[102] *ibid., per* McHugh and Gummow J.J., 77 A.L.J.R. 1312 at 1327–1328; 199 A.L.R. 131 at 151–152, citing Lord Millett in *Mcfarlane, op. cit.,* n. 93 above, at 108.

[103] *ibid.,* 77 A.L.J.R. 1312 at 1336–1337; 199 A.L.R. 131 at 164.

[104] *ibid.,* 77 A.L.J.R. 1312 at 1369; 199 A.L.R. 131 at 209; cf. *Crawford El v Britton* (1998) 523 U.S. 574, *per* Rehnquist J., at 606–609 (diss) cited *Lasser, op. cit.,* n. 59 above, at 883.

issues of legal and public policy that may influence their decisions in particular cases?

One reason for the change in the judicial method is clearly the impact that legal realists have had on judicial thinking in the common law world since Pound, his pupil in Australia Julius Stone, and their successors, taught the unsettling truth that law, expressed in words, is often uncertain and ambiguous. Syllogistic reasoning and "excessive legalism" may "flatter that longing for certainty and for repose which is in every human mind". But, according to Holmes, comfortable certainty in the law it is all too often "an illusion and repose is not the destiny of man".[105]

Later American jurists would tell us that the quest for certainty and strict logic was born of an infantile desire to restore in the world at large the unquestioning obedience to omniscience and omnipotence that we attributed in infancy to our parents.[106] However that may be, and whether the denial of the role of policy in judicial decision-making is the product of romantic illusions[107] or just the imperatives of rigidly conservative-leaning elderly men,[108] decades of instruction about the psychology of decision-making[109] and analysis of the inherent obscurities of language as the vehicle for legal ideas, have made contemporary judges much more understanding of the choices that they face in resolving the legal disputes that come before them. In the nature of things, appellate courts tend to get more than their fair share of difficult cases. Final, and constitutional, courts get the most difficult problems.[110] Against the background of such truths, the presentation of a decision as if it arose entirely from an analysis of the language of past decisions, clothed in strict logic, is less likely to be satisfying now than

---

[105] O.W.Holmes Jr., "The Path of the Law" (1897) 10 *Harvard Law Review* 457 at p. 465; R. L. Brooks, "The Use of Policy in Judicial Reasoning: A Reconceptualization Before and After *Bush v Gore*" (2002) 13 *Stanford L. & Pol. Rev.* 33 at pp. 37–38.

[106] M.D.Kirby, "Judging: Reflections on the Moment of Decision" (1999) 18 *Australian Bar Review* 4, p. 19 citing Judge Jerome Frank, *Law and the Modern Mind* (Bretano's, New York, 1931), pp. 3, 13, 267ff.

[107] Brooks, *op. cit.*, n. 105 above, pp. 33–34 by reference to the experiences of Stevens J. in his first year on the Supreme Court of the United States as recounted in B. Woodward and S. Armstrong, *The Brethren—Inside the Supreme Court* (Simon and Schuster, New York, 1979), p. 443.

[108] M.Kozlowski, *The Myth of the Imperial Judiciary* (N.Y.U. Press, New York, 2003), p. 219.

[109] Kirby, *op. cit.*, n. 106 above, at pp. 19–20.

[110] J.Walker, "Judicial Tendencies in Statutory Construction: Differing Views on the Role of the Judge" (2001) 58 *New York University Annual Survey of American Law*, 2001 203 at p. 203.

once it was. This is so for the judge, the legal profession and the informed community.

After the spell of "excessive legalism" was broken in the last quarter of the twentieth century, persistence in the "noble lie" could deceive no one for long. Once judges, in particular cases, began to identify the imperatives of legal policy in their reasoning, the fiction that they had decided a novel case without regard to relevant principles and policy would cut little ice.[111] Indeed, the pretence that judges had decided important and difficult questions by reference solely to a verbal analysis of things written in different cases (often in a different time, from different perspectives and with different background knowledge) is likely to alarm knowledgeable lawyers and other citizens now aware of the discussion that will have gone on behind the scenes.

The central issue in the debate over judicial activism is not, therefore, the judge's personal preferences and prejudices (although they may be hard enough to escape). It is, in Herbert Hart's words, the true and "conscientious exploration" wherever existing legal authority proves inadequate, of the *real* "bases for their dispositions".[112] Unless judges disclose those "bases" of legal principle and legal policy, their reasons will not only be less honest but also less convincing. The reasons will be more obscure to the public and to other lawyers because they have set out to hide relevant considerations behind a pretence of legal formalism.[113] More worrying still, they may mask illogical and unprincipled decision-making, even from the decision-maker.[114] Without identifying relevant issues of legal principle and legal policy, there is a real risk that the judge may be unaware of them or be content to stumble along from case to case in a confusion of ideas derived from a purely verbal analysis of past authority without appropriate regard to the dynamics of the new context in which the propounded rules must operate.

[111] B.Horrigan, "Paradigm Shifts in Judicial Interpretation: Reframing Legal and Constitutional Reasoning" in *Interpreting Constitutions—Theories, Principles and Institutions* (C. Sampford and K. Preston eds., Federation Press, Sydney, 1996) p. 31 at pp. 71–73; B. Galligan, *Politics of the High Court* (Uni Qld Press, 1987), p. 251.

[112] A.B.Handler, "Judging Public Policy" (2000) 31 *Rutgers Law Journal* 301 at p. 308 citing H. L. A. Hart, *The Concept of Law* (Clarendon Press, Oxford, 1961), p. 593.

[113] cf. S.Todd, "Negligence and Policy" in *The Struggle for Simplicity in the Law—Essays for Lord Cooke of Thorndon* (P. Rishworth ed., Butterworths, Wellington, 1997) p. 105 at p. 110.

[114] Friendly, *op. cit.*, n. 82 above, at p. 290.

TELLING IT AS IT IS

Apart from the foregoing considerations that make adherence to the techniques of strict legalism unattractive to many contemporary judges and lawyers of the common law, there is another reason for the shift of legal doctrine. This is the desire of many leaders of the judiciary to ditch the "noble lie" and to explain what actually happens in practice in reaching a judicial conclusion.

In 1997, Lord Bingham explained that the notion that judges merely "declare" a pre-existing law, deriving it by strict logic from past precedent, "was inconsistent with the subjective experience of judges, particularly appellate judges, of the role they fulfilled day by day".[115] "They know", he declared, "and the higher the court the more right they are, that decisions involve issues of policy".

A quarter century earlier, Lord Denning said much the same in *Dutton v Bognor Regis UDC*:

> "It seems to me that it is a question of policy we, as judges, have to decide . . . We should decide . . . according to the reason of the thing . . . [W]hat is the best policy for the law to adopt? . . . [T]he question has always been there in the background. It has been concealed behind such questions as: Was the defendant under any duty to the plaintiff?, Was the relationship sufficiently proximate?, Was the injury direct or indirect? . . . Nowadays we direct ourselves to the considerations of policy".[116]

Accepting these truths does not mean that a judge is free to give effect to purely personal values. Without under-estimating the importance of subjective perceptions, the values of legal principle and legal policy must be extracted from a wide range of sources larger than the judge's *own* values. They include any relevant constitutional text, applicable statutory provisions and judicial decisions on analogous points. Whilst serious risks can arise in judicial attempts to derive a higher legal principle from a multitude of past cases, or to expound each and every consideration of policy that affects the expression of a new rule of the common law, there are even greater risks in attempting to return to "strict and complete legalism". Sir Anthony Mason, a

---

[115] Lord Bingham of Cornhill, "The Judge as Lawmaker: An English Perspective" in *The Struggle for Simplicity in the Law—Essays for Lord Cooke of Thorndon* (P. Rishworth ed., Butterworths, Wellington, 1997), p. 3 at p. 6.

[116] [1972] 1 Q.B. 373 at 397. See also Lord Cooke of Thorndon, "The New Zealand National Legal Identity" (1987) 3 *Canterbury Law Review* 171.

past Chief Justice of Australia, has rightly described such an attempt as one presenting a dangerous "cloak for undisclosed and unidentified policy values".[117]

What follows? Obviously, it would be wrong for a judge to set out in pursuit of a personal policy agenda and hang the law. But it would also be wrong, and futile, for the judge to pretend that the solutions to all of the complex problems of the law today, unresolved by incontestably clear and applicable texts, can be by the application of nothing more than purely verbal reasoning and strict logic to words written by judges in earlier times about the problems they then faced.

Once judges acknowledge the reality of choice they are duty-bound, in their reasons, to accept the obligation of explaining the considerations that have led them to select one decision over another.[118] Once it is accepted that, in many problems reaching appellate courts, there is more than one possible answer to a disputed point of law, it is difficult to avoid the conclusion that a reason for providing a second level of appeal is precisely to permit a more mature consideration of the policy directions of the law. It is not simply to go over again the work done in the intermediate court.[119] Honesty that this is so helps to transform the debate that follows into a consideration not only of the elements of past authority but also of relevant considerations of principle and policy. True, this is a process that should remain "tethered" to authoritative texts. But it should be kept on a loose rein so that the decision-maker can explore any new considerations that will help protect the applicable law from atrophy, injustice or irrelevance.[120]

It is by resolving the tension between these dual aspects of its nature that the law, in Roscoe Pound's words, is stable, although it cannot stand still.[121] Even judges who wish it were otherwise cannot ignore the imperatives of legal policy. In many, if not most, appellate cases there is no real alternative.[122] So long as human language remains imprecise and human capacity to predict the future limited, it will fall to judges to fill

---

[117] A.F.Mason, "The Role of a Constitutional Court in a Federation: A Comparison of the Australian and the United States Experience" (1986) 16 *Federal Law Review* 1 at p. 5. See also A. F. Mason, "Future Directions in Australian Law" (1987) 13 *Monash University Law Review* 149 at pp. 155–156.

[118] Kozlowski, *op. cit.*, n. 108 above, p. 219; J. Raskin, *Overruling Democracy: The Supreme Court versus The American People* (Routledge, New York, 2003), p. 241.

[119] Atiyah, *op. cit.*, n. 80 above, p. 157.

[120] Doyle, *op. cit.*, n. 7 above, at p. 93.

[121] R.Pound, *Interpretations of Legal History* (C.U.P., Cambridge, 1923), p. 1.

[122] Friendly, *op. cit.*, n. 82, above at p. 290.

the gaps in the law's rules. They will do so, as they should, by reference to considerations of principle and policy.[123] Better that they should tell it as it is.

STATUTORY CONSTRUCTION

The common law today orbits in a universe of statute. Most of the work of modern judges, including appellate judges, involves giving meaning to the language of legislation, including (where they exist) a written constitution and human rights instruments incorporated into domestic law.

These documents, expressed in imperative language that must be discovered and explained for the particular case, present challenges that are somewhat different from the controversies arising over the contents of the common law itself. They have this much in common. The rules of each system—statute and judge-made law—are expressed in language. The English language is specially rich in ambiguity because of its mixture of Germanic and Latin influences. The sources of the written law's commands may be more confined. However, the problems of ambiguity and choice are the same. In recognition of such choices, rules of construction have been devised by courts and by the legislature itself. Attempts to express legislation in "plain English" have produced new questions. With the recognition of the choices that judges face in common law elaboration has come a clearer recognition of the scope for choice that lies in legislative construction. The move towards a more purposive interpretation of legislation mirrors, in turn, the changes that have happened in judicial decision-making in contested decisions about the common law.[124]

In the United Kingdom[125] the principle of purposive construction of legislation which has gradually replaced the previous rule of literal interpretation that had enjoyed general

---

[123] Handler, *op. cit.*, n. 112 above, at p. 305; cf. *Grobbelaar v News Group Newspapers Ltd* [2002] 1 W.L.R. 3024, *per* Lord Steyn, at 3040.

[124] A.F.Mason, "Changing the Law in a Changing Society" (1993) 67 *Australian Law Journal* 568 at p. 569; cf. I. Callinan, "An Over-Mighty Court?" (1994) 4 *Proceedings of the Samuel Griffith Society* 81 at p. 90.

[125] *Jones v Wrotham Park Settled Estates* [1980] A.C. 74, *per* Lord Diplock, at 105; *Exxon Corporation v Exxon Insurance Consultants International Ltd* [1982] Ch. 119 *per* Oliver L.J., at 144; See also Lord Diplock, "The Courts as Legislators" in *The Lawyer and Justice* (B. Harvey ed., Sweet and Maxwell, London, 1978) at p. 274; *Fothergill v Monarch Airlines Ltd* [1981] A.C. 251, *per* Lord Wilberforce, at 272–273, 275; *per* Lord Diplock, at 280; *per* Lord Scarman, at 291.

acceptance for more than a century. The latter reflected many of the same features of the mechanical view of the judicial function found in the declaratory theory of common law elaboration.[126] Like the English courts and courts of most countries of the common law tradition, the High Court of Australia has also adopted a purposive approach.[127] That approach was recently affirmed by the entire Court.[128] Of course, in a particular case a purposive approach may be agreed yet the judges may disagree about what precisely that purpose is.

Inherent in this shift in the approach to statutory construction is the enlargement of the acknowledged role of the judge in ascertaining what the purpose or policy of the legislation is, in order to help give effect to it.[129] Any literate person can read an Act. Armed with a dictionary or two,[130] such a person can give the words their literal meaning. However, recognition of the fact that interpretation is a more complex function, in which the judicial decision-maker is more than a mechanic, sits comfortably with the contemporary acknowledgment of the creative function of the judge in ascertaining and applying the common law and the modern rules of equity.

In the United Kingdom, the Human Rights Act 1998 (UK) has extended the boundaries of purposive interpretation because of the instruction which that Act contains to afford statutory language a meaning that is conformable with the European Convention on Human Rights. Indeed the judges are enjoined by that Act to adopt such an interpretation so long as this is "possible".[131] There is nothing quite like this direction in Australia—or anywhere else to my knowledge. If such a statutory formula were attempted in Australia, a question might arise as to whether it was constitutionally permissible for the Parliament to give such an instruction to the courts. A party on the receiving end might complain that such a stretching of the meaning of the authoritative text (where a construction is

---

[126] M.D.Kirby, "Towards a Grand Theory of Interpretation: The Case of Statutes and Contracts" (2003) 242 *Statute Law Review* 95 where the cases are collected.

[127] *Kingston v Keprose Pty Ltd* (1987) 11 N.S.W.L.R. 404 *per* McHugh J. (diss), at 423–424, approved *Bropho v Western Australia* (1990) 171 C.L.R. 1 *per* Mason C.J., Deane, Dawson, Toohey, Gaudron and McHugh J.J., at 20; *Project Blue Sky Inc v Australian Broadcasting Authority* (1998) 194 C.L.R. 355, *per* McHugh, Gummow, Kirby and Hayne J.J., at 381–382.

[128] *Eastman v Director of Public Prosecutions* (ACT) (2003) 77 A.L.J.R. 1122, *per* McHugh J., at 1127; *per* Heydon J., at 1150; 198 A.L.R. 1 at 8, 39.

[129] *Nelson, op. cit.*, n. 77 above, *per* McHugh J.

[130] *Regina v Secretary of State for Health; Ex parte Quintavalle (on behalf of Pro-Life Alliance)* [2003] 2 AC 687, *per* Lord Steyn at 700.

[131] Human Rights Act, s. 3.

"possible" but not preferable) does not conform to an impartial exercise of the judicial power. Fortunately, that question does not arise for me to decide.

For present purposes, it is enough to point to the inherently *creative* role that the function of statutory interpretation affords to a judge, even in the case of prosaic legislation.[132] It is a role with necessary limits.[133] Sometimes the command of legislation will appear to be clear and unambiguous. However, words in statutes often give rise to contradictory interpretations. Such differences can sometimes be traced to the different perceptions which the judges hold of the legislative purpose, as ascertained from the language, history, background documents and apparent policy of the law.[134]

Evident in the differences that can arise between individual judges in the construction of statutory language are disagreements very similar to those that have emerged in the controversies over the judicial method in expressing the common law. Those who are less inclined to see in earlier precedents a principle that will afford a platform for expressing a new common law right or duty may be equally resistant to construing a statute so as to ensure that it hits its presumed target where the words are less than ideal. In this situation judges will sometimes explain their disinclination to adapt the statutory language by reference to their deference to the legislature.[135] Yet to those of the opposite view, the "restraint" of their colleagues may be viewed as a formalistic indifference to the function of the judge in mediating the attainment of just outcomes that accord with the perceived legislative purpose. Such judges will assert that the legislature assumes that interpreters will draw necessary inferences; and that it expects relevant aspects of legal policy to be applied because a statute is never intended to operate in a vacuum but as part of the whole body of the law.[136]

The growth of legislation as the main source of contemporary law alters the role of the contemporary judge of the common

---

[132] *Quintavalle, op. cit.,* n. 130 above *per* Lord Bingham, at 695.

[133] *Macdonald v Ministry of Defence* [2003] I.C.R. 937, *per* Lord Nicholls, at 943. Lord Devlin was less willing to allow creativity where Parliament had spoken than where the matter was entirely one for judge-made law: P. Devlin, "Judges and Lawmakers" (1976) 39 *Modern Law Review* 1, at p. 13. However, this view reflected the earlier literalist approach to statutory interpretation which he defended.

[134] H.M.Hart Jr. and A. M. Sacks, *The Legal Process: Basic Problems in the Making and Application of Law* (Federation Press, Boston, 1994) cited in Walker, *op. cit.,* n. 110 above, at p. 213. For a United States illustration see *Eastern Associated Coal Corp v United Mine Workers of America* 531 U.S. 57 (2000).

[135] *e.g. Gustafson v Alloyed Co.* 513 U.S. 561, *per curiam,* at 573 (1995).

[136] Bennion, *op. cit.,* n. 52 above, p. 657.

law. In giving effect to legislative purposes, the judge today, with or without a human rights charter, will commonly view the legislative command through a perspective of human rights law or equivalent principle. In countries like my own (still without a comprehensive bill of rights) the applicable norms will, more often than not, be ascertained in terms of the basic common law rights of the individual.[137] Often the result will not be so different from that reached in countries with enforceable human rights standards.

Recently, in a case involving ambiguous federal legislation, the High Court of Australia followed the decision of the House of Lords in *R. (Morgan Grenfell and Co Ltd) v Special Commissioner of Income Tax*.[138] The question in the Australian case was whether a legislative provision had abrogated legal professional privilege so as to allow a government agency to demand access to documents in the possession of the solicitors for a corporation then under investigation for breach of the Trade Practices Act 1974 (Cth). A literal interpretation of the Act might have upheld the claim of the governmental agency to have the documents.[139] But the Court unanimously concluded that, if Parliament intended to take away the important right to confidential legal advice, including in the case of a corporation, it was obliged to make its purpose clear and unmistakable. In short, Parliament had to wear the political opprobrium and assume the accountability to the community which such a course entailed. It should not be left to a court to infer such a serious purpose from the statutory text.

The scope for the judicial interpretation of legislation in a way that avoids unjustifiable discrimination, upholds human rights but still gives effect to the language in question may be seen in many modern cases. In *Fitzpatrick v Sterling Housing Association Limited*,[140] the House of Lords, by majority, held that a same-sex partner was a member of the "family" of the deceased lessee. As such, he was entitled to succeed to the deceased's entitlements under the *Rents Act*.[141] However, the decision divided

---

[137] *Potter v Minahan* (1908) 7 C.L.R. 277, *per* O'Connor J., at 304; *Ex parte Walsh and Johnson; In re Yates* (1925) 37 C.L.R. 36, *per* Isaacs J., at 93; *Bropho, op. cit.*, n. 127 above, *per* Mason C.J., Deane, Dawson, Toohey, Gaudron and McHugh J.J., at 18; *Daniels Corporation v Australian Competition and Consumer Commission* (2002) 77 A.L.J.R. 40, *per* Gleeson C.J., Gaudron, Gummow and Hayne J.J., at 43; *per* McHugh J., at 49; *per* Kirby J., at 57; 192 A.L.R. 561 at 561, 565, 573, 584–585.

[138] [2003] 1 A.C. 563.

[139] *Daniels, op. cit.*, n. 137 above; cf. *Esso Australia Resources Ltd v Federal Commissioner of Taxation* (1999) 201 C.L.R. 49.

[140] [2001] 1 A.C. 27.

[141] *ibid., per* Lord Slynn, at 40, *per* Lord Nicholls, at 46–47, *per* Lord Clyde, at 54–55.

their Lordships. It involved the adoption of an interpretation of the statutory language that would not have been accepted twenty or more years ago. This fact indicates the role that judges play in applying the law justly, so as to avoid discrimination contrary to contemporary perceptions of human dignity.[142] In acting in such a way, a court presumes that the legislature would not intend to act in a discriminatory manner without clear language requiring such an outcome. This is a noble assumption that attributes to Parliament decent motivations. One suspects that, as in *Fitzpatrick*, it sometimes rests on a fiction as much as on political realities.

It is not enough that judges should uphold the basic legal rights of large, well represented corporations. Judges in today's world must also stand guardian for the rights of minorities and of the vulnerable in society.[143] Advances in the understanding of the judicial role over the past twenty years make it impossible to return to the techniques of literalist interpretation of statute law.[144] This conclusion makes it equally unlikely that, under the pressure of a Counter-Reformation, the judiciary will revert to a rule of formalism in ascertaining the contents of the common law.[145]

CONSTITUTIONAL INTERPRETATION

If choices must be made in the interpretation of an ordinary statute, the elucidation of written constitutions presents the problem of choice writ on a larger canvas. Typically, written constitutions are difficult to alter. They contain the law under which other laws are made. Conventionally, they divide the power of government between different organs and polities. Today, they normally contain a list of fundamental rights which it is left to judges to interpret and apply.

The function of constitutional interpretation is inescapably political. Sir Owen Dixon would not have denied it.[146] Indeed, it was the very political character of the role of the High Court of Australia in applying the federal Constitution and keeping the

---

[142] See also *Re W (A Minor) (Adoption: Homosexual Adopter)* [1997] 3 W.L.R. 768, *per* Singer J., at 774; *Nelson, op. cit.*, n. 77 above, *per* Toohey J., at 585–597.
[143] Guarnieri and Pederzoli, *op. cit.*, n. 57 above, p. 187. See *Attorney-General (WA) v Marquet* [2003] 78 ALJR 105, *per* Kirby J, at 125–138; 202 ALR 233, at 274–279.
[144] As was held in *Macdonald, op. cit.*, above n. 133, *per* Lord Nicholls, at [17]; cf. A. M. Gleeson, "Judicial Legitimacy" (2000) 20 *Australian Bar Review* 4 at p. 7.
[145] Atiyah, *op. cit.*, n. 80 above, p. 154.
[146] *Melbourne Corporation v The Commonwealth* (1947) 74 C.L.R. 31 at 82.

federal balance between the Commonwealth and the States that led Dixon to insist on what he called "strict legalism". There was no other way, according to him, that a court of judges could maintain the confidence of the opinionated and powerful interests typically lined up in great constitutional disputes.[147]

Occasionally, we still hear resonances of "strict legalism".[148] An important decision of the High Court of Australia in 1999 held that sensible integrated State laws permitting the transfer ("cross-vesting") of state cases to federal courts where the federal venue was more appropriate were constitutionally invalid. The laws had been enacted in a cooperative scheme adopted by every Australian legislature. Defending the laws, the State and Federal Governments referred to the utility of the legislative arrangement which had operated successfully over ten years. They appealed to a fundamental assumption of intergovernmental cooperation within the Australian federation. They asserted that such co-operation was inherent in the constitutional text. However, the Court, by majority, reversed the opinion that had prevailed in an earlier evenly divided decision of the Court upholding the laws.[149] With the support of the opinions of three newly appointed judges, the laws were held to be unconstitutional. A vital part of the sensible scheme of cross-vesting collapsed. Two of the majority judges criticised the reference to notions of constitutional cooperation. They called for a return to "legal analysis"[150]:

> "Characterising a set of circumstances as having an Australian rather than a local flavour or as a desirable response to the complexity of a modern national society is to use perceived convenience as a criterion of constitutional validity instead of legal analysis and the application of accepted constitutional doctrine".

Such words are no longer received as uncritically in Australia as they would have been in the era of Sir Owen Dixon. A leading Australian constitutional law scholar, Professor Leslie Zines, pointed out that the nature of a written constitution, and the typical brevity of its language, imposes on the court the responsibility of construing and applying the text, a task that travels far beyond purely verbal analysis.

---

[147] Dixon, *op. cit.*, n. 35 above, at p. xiv.
[148] Heydon, *op. cit.*, n. 37 above, at pp. 113–116.
[149] *Gould v Brown* (1998) 193 C.L.R. 346.
[150] *Re Wakim; Ex parte McNally* (1999) 198 C.L.R. 511, *per* Gummow and Hayne J.J., at 581–582. *Marquet, op. cit.*, n. 143 above, 78 A.L.J.R. 105, *per* Gleeson CJ, Gummow, Hayne and Heydon J.J., at 114; cf. *per* Kirby J., at 137; 202 A.L.R. 233, at 245, 277–278.

Yet even in the days of Sir Owen Dixon's dominance, the High Court of Australia was not reluctant, when it mattered, to reaching conclusions based upon implications drawn by the judges from the structure and purpose of the Constitution, although not spelt out in its terms.[151] This was their choice and it was a legal choice. In one of the finest decisions of the Australian Court, given in 1951, it invalidated a federal law that had sought to ban the Communist Party and to attach numerous civil disabilities to people "declared" by the Executive to be communists.[152] In explaining his conclusion that the law was constitutionally invalid, Dixon relied on a broad political and philosophical notion of the rule of law. He treated this as a fundamental "assumption" of the Constitution. He held that it helped to determine the outer boundary of federal legislative power which had been exceeded.

In another, still controversial, decision Dixon led a majority of the High Court of Australia to invalidate the law establishing a federal industrial court that had existed for more than fifty years. The function of that Court to arbitrate industrial disputes in awards having prospective operation was held to mix judicial and non-judicial power impermissibly. This, the court majority found, was forbidden not by an *express* textual prohibition.[153] Instead, it was incompatible with the *structure* of the Constitution. This conclusion required Dixon—the great defender of "strict legalism"—to infer the presence in the Constitution of rules that were not spelt out explicitly in the document's text.

There were other decisions of the Dixon years based on perceived constitutional implications.[154] Although additional constitutional implications continue to be found by Dixon's successors,[155] the issue remains controversial amongst doctrinal hard-liners. They find it difficult to accept as a constitutional

---

[151] L.Zines, "Legalism, Realism and Judicial Rhetoric in Constitutional Law" (Byers Lecture) (2002) *NSW Bar Notes* 13.

[152] *Australian Communist Party v The Commonwealth* (1951) 83 C.L.R. 1 at 193.

[153] *The Queen v Kirby; Ex parte Boilermakers' Society of Australia* (1956) 94 C.L.R. 254 (HCA) ("*Boilermakers' case*").

[154] Zines, *op. cit.*, above n. 151, at 13 referring to *Melbourne Corporation v The Commonwealth* (1947) 74 C.L.R. 31 at 83; *Parton v Milk Board* (1949) 80 C.L.R. 229 at 260.

[155] *e.g.* an implied limitation on the enactment of laws interfering in free communication on matters of political and economic concern (*Lange v Australian Broadcasting Corporation* (1997) 189 C.L.R. 520); an implied limitation on interference with the independence of State courts (*Kable v Director of Public Prosecutions (NSW)* (1997) 189 C.L.R. 51); and an implied limitation on the imposition of certain federal taxes on the remuneration of State judges (*Austin v The Commonwealth* (2003) 77 A.L.J.R. 491; 195 A.L.R. 321).

command anything that is not expressed in clear terms. Some even doubt any approach to constitutional meaning that strays from the intentions of the original Founding Fathers of the Constitution.

There have been similar disputes in Canada, especially since the *Charter of Rights and Freedoms* was added to that country's Constitution. Critics from left and right have attacked the *Charter* as neither philosophically nor democratically workable. They have criticised the Supreme Court for its decisions on the *Charter*. On the other hand, surveys of popular opinion suggest a generally high level of public satisfaction with the decisions of the Canadian Court.[156] Opponents of the constitutionalisation of rights in Canada regard the *Charter* as proof of a failure of democracy. Supporters, on the other hand, claim that its success has promoted a more active debate over civic values and a strengthening of political and legal institutions and of constitutionalism itself.

The acute needs of the developing countries of the Commonwealth have sometimes produced an approach to constitutional interpretation that is unashamedly described as "activist", including by judges themselves. Thus in India, at least in most legal circles, the phrase "judicial activism" is not viewed as one of condemnation.[157] So urgent and numerous are the needs of that society that anything else would be regarded by many— including many judges and lawyers—as an abdication of the final court's essential constitutional role.

One instance may be cited from Indian experience: the expansion of the traditional notion of standing to sue in public interest litigation.[158] The Indian Supreme Court has upheld the right of prisoners, the poor and other vulnerable groups to enlist its constitutional jurisdiction by simply sending a letter to the Court.[159] This might not seem appropriate in a developed

---

[156] I.Binnie, "The Future of Equality", Paper for a Conference on Liberty, Equality, Community: Constitutional Rights in Conflict? (Auckland, 1999). See M.D.Kirby, "Constitutional Interpretation and Original Intent: A Form of Ancestor Worship?" (2000) 24 *University of Melbourne Law Review* 1 at p. 2.

[157] V.Kumar, "Constitutional Democracy and Judicial Activism" in *India: 50 Years of Independence* (V. Grover and R. Arora eds., 1997), p. 205. See also J. Narayan, "Judicial Activism and Protection of Human Rights in India" (2001) 3 *Journal of Constitutional and Parliamentary Studies* 111 at p. 116; and T. Zwart, Review (2003) 30 *Journal of Law & Society* 332.

[158] Discussed in M.D.Kirby, "Judicial Activism" (1997) 27 *University of Western Australian Law Review* 1.

[159] *Gupta v President of India* (1982) 69 A.I.R. S.C. 149, *per* Bhagwati J., at 152; U. Baxi, "Taking Suffering Seriously: Social Action Litigation in the Supreme

country. Yet it appears perfectly adapted to the nation to which the Indian Constitution speaks. Lord Chief Justice Woolf recently confessed to having been astounded at first by the proactive approach of the Indian Supreme Court in this and other respects. However, he went on:[160]

> ". . . I soon realised that if that Court was to perform its essential role in Indian society, it had no option but to adopt the course it did and I congratulate it for the courage it has shown".

A demand addressed to Indian judges that they return to "excessive legalism" and verbal formalism would be considered by most of them with astonishment tinged with derision. Rejected in other fields of law, such an approach would be regarded as specially inappropriate to the interpretation of a living constitution. Particularly would this be so with respect to broadly stated human rights provisions contained in the Indian Constitution.

In the United States, with the oldest written Constitution still in force, there are strong proponents of formalism, literalism and interpretation according to the "original intent" of the Founders who wrote the Constitution. No judge of that Court has been more vigorous in defending that approach than Justice Antonin Scalia.[161] However, for the moment, his approach appears to have been eclipsed by other opinions. In *Lawrence v Texas*,[162] decided in June 2003, the Court, by majority, struck down as contrary to the Equal Protection and Due Process clauses of the Eighth and Fourteenth Amendments, the provisions of a Texas law criminalising adult, consensual, private homosexual conduct. In his reasons for the Court, Justice Kennedy explained the approach which the majority favoured:

> "Had those who drew and ratified the Due Process Clauses of the Fifth Amendment or the Fourteenth Amendment known the components of liberty in its manifold possibilities, they might have been

Court of India" (1980) 9 *Delhi Law Review* 91; *Bandhua Mukti Morcha v Union of India* (1984) 71 A.I.R. S.C. 802, *per* Bhagwati J., at 813; *Mehta v Union of India* (1987) 74 A.I.R. S.C. 1086, *per* Bhagwati C.J., at 1089.
[160] Lord Woolf of Barnes, "The International Role of the Judiciary", unpublished paper, Commonwealth Law Conference, Melbourne, April 2003 available at: *www.lcd.gov.uk/judicial/speeches/lcj160403.htm*.
[161] A.Scalia, *A Matter of Interpretation: Federal Courts and the Law*, (Princeton University Press, Princeton, 1997), p. 47; cf. G.Craven, "The High Court of Australia: A Study in the Abuse of Power" (1999) *University of New South Wales Law Journal* 216 at p. 225; Walker, *op. cit.*, n. 110 above, pp. 235–236.
[162] 71 U.S.L.W. 4574 (2003).

more specific. They did not presume to have this insight. They knew times can blind us to certain truths and later generations can see that laws once thought necessary and proper in fact serve only to oppress. As the Constitution endures, persons in every generation can invoke its principles in their own search for greater freedom".[163]

This is an approach to the task of constitutional interpretation identical to my own.[164] It derives from the essential function which a written constitution is expected to fulfil. Construing a constitution with a catchcry about "legalism", with nothing more than judicial case books and a dictionary to help, and with no concept of the way it is intended to operate in the nation whose people accept it as their basic law, is a contemptible idea. As one anonymous sage once put it: if you construe a constitution like a last will and testament, that is what it will become.

Happily, despite the comfortable but deceptive rhetoric about "strict legalism", this is not the way the Australian Constitution, or most other such documents, have been interpreted in countries of the common law tradition.[165] Fortunately, in Britain too, the leading judges have rejected the "straight-jacket of legal logic". They have dismissed that approach as an inadequate guide for the interpretation of human rights and other constitutional laws.[166]

Nevertheless, legal reasoning, unlike political activism, must always remain attached to legal authority. Consistency and the avoidance of purely personal idiosyncrasies require that tasks of interpretation commence with any relevant texts and proceed with the assistance of any applicable legal history. In important constitutional cases, and especially where novel issues are presented, such sources are insufficient. They do not take the mind of the decision-maker far enough along the journey to the decision. I agree with Professor Leslie Zines:

---

[163] *ibid.*, *per* Kennedy J. (with whom Stevens, Souter, Ginsburg, and Breyer J.J., concurred), at 4580. O'C.onnor J. gave a separate concurring opinion.

[164] *Re Wakim*, *op. cit.*, n. 150 above, at 599–600; *Grain Pool of Western Australia v The Commonwealth* (2000) 202 C.L.R. 479 at 522–523.

[165] A recent illustration concerns the constitutional status of British nationality in Australia. In 1901, Australian nationality was that of "subject of the Queen" (*Australian Constitution*, s. 117). However, by 1999 such a subject, who was a British, but not an Australian, citizen, was held "under . . . allegiance . . . to a foreign power" within s. 44(i) of the *Constitution: Sue v Hill* (1999) 199 C.L.R. 462. See also *Nolan v Minister of State for Immigration and Ethnic Affairs* (1988) 165 C.L.R. 178 and *Re Patterson; Ex parte Taylor* (2001) 207 C.L.R. 391; and *Shaw v Minister for Immigration and Multicultural Affairs* (2003) 78 A.L.J.R. 203; 203 A.L.R. 143.

[166] Lord Steyn, "Democracy Through Law", (Robin Cooke Lecture, 2002) (2002) 6 *European Human Rights Law Review* 723.

"Constitutions . . . continue to open up situations where judges must choose between equally rational conclusions that cannot be settled by doctrine or precedent alone. In an age of open government it is important that, whatever the new legalism means, judicial conclusions should not be seen as simply resting on different perceptions or impressions, but examined in the light of consequences and appropriate policies. This may come down to regarding law as a means of fulfilling social ends rather than as an end in itself".[167]

In finding the applicable rule of the common law or of equity, in choosing the preferable meaning of a contested statutory text and, above all, in construing the words of a constitutional document, judges have choices. One of the greatest advances in my legal lifetime has been the realization and acknowledgement that this is so. It has led to a generation of judges who are more truthful about the choices they make. This has truly been a great legal Reformation. The change that it wrought was especially notable in Australia where the doctrine of "strict and complete legalism" had earlier rejected such thoughts as legal heresy.

But now a Counter-Reformation has begun. It has attracted some powerful exponents. It cannot be ignored. It will be the subject of my third lecture.

[167] Zines, *op. cit.*, n. 151 above, p. 19.

3. Counter-Reformation

RETURN TO THE FAIRYTALE

Until recently most knowledgeable observers considered that it was Lord Reid, the Scot, who delivered the *coup de grace* to the doctrine of legal formalism. He laughed at it. At the time, many of us thought that it had sunk, never to be seen again, under the weight of his noble laughter.

Reid had not been the first judge in modern times to scold the "lack of candour" in the conventional expositions of the judicial method. More than half a century before Reid's salvo, Benjamin Cardozo, then a judge of the New York Court of Appeals, had suggested that the obfuscation of the judicial method derived from a judicial fear that judges would "lose respect and confidence by the reminder that they are subject to human limitations".[168] If it became known that judges made determinations according to policy considerations, they might, Cardozo feared, risk losing "the grandeur of the conception that lifts them into the realm of pure reasoning". They might be shown "not [to] stand aloof on these chill and distant heights". For all the risks, Cardozo concluded that judges "shall not help the cause of truth by acting and speaking as if they do [stand aloof]". He urged a hearty dose of the truth. He was sure that the judicial institution would survive it.

Perhaps because of the studied eloquence of his writing, Cardozo's views did not have the impact, at least in Commonwealth countries, of Lord Reid's robust dismissal of the old mythology about the judicial method. This is what Reid wrote:[169]

"There was a time when it was thought almost indecent to suggest that judges make law . . . Those with a taste for fairytales seem to

---

[168] B.Cardozo, *The Nature of the Judicial Process* (Yale University Press, New Haven, 1921), p. 168; cf. Kozlowski, *op. cit.*, n. 108 above, p. 220.
[169] Lord Reid, "The Judge as Lawmaker" (1972) 12 *Journal of Society of Public Teachers of Law* 23; cf. M. D. Kirby, *The Judges* (Boyer Lectures, 1983) (Australian Broadcasting Commission, Sydney, 1983), p. 59.

have thought that in some Aladdin's cave there is hidden the Common Law in all its splendour and that on a judge's appointment there descends on him knowledge of the magic words Open Sesame. Bad decisions are given when the judge has muddled the password and the wrong door opens. But we do not believe in fairytales any more".

Responding to the new realism demanded by Reid and others of like mind, the legal Reformation dawned in virtually every country of the common law. Encouraged by it, judges recognised, and acknowledged, the inescapable complexity of their work. They identified the choices they had to make. And they began to spell out the considerations of legal principle and legal policy that helped them to express the governing law for a particular case, thereby resolving doubts and ambiguities in any relevant legal authority.

The Old Testament was closed and a new era of candour opened as judges of the legal Reformation sought to formulate a new and more honest methodology that did not pretend that finding the applicable rule was possible by a purely verbal analysis or by the "strict logic and high technique" earlier claimed by Justice Dixon and those of like opinion.

In many countries, the enlightenment of the legal Reformation continues to this day. In the United Kingdom, the present leaders of the judiciary are amongst its most formidable exponents.[170] Yet just as we were feeling safe in this new era and excited at the challenge of elaborating a new judicial method, a Counter-Reformation was launched by old style formalists. The chief object of these lectures is to give a warning about the strategies of those who lead the call to return the law to the land of intellectual fairytales. Law's nature tends to be conservative. A call to return to the comfortable world of past myths and fictions has a seductive attractiveness for many lawyers. Those who have welcomed, and followed, the new judicial method must therefore be on their guard, lest the legal Counter-Reformation succeeded in gaining converts by stealth.

The expression "judicial activism" need not have been a pejorative label.[171] If Cardozo, Reid and other realists were right in their assessments of what judges actually do, "activism" of a sort was the very essence of the judicial method of the common

---

[170] Lord Bingham, *op. cit.*, n. 115 above; Lord Steyn, *op. cit.*, n. 166 above; Lord Woolf, *op. cit.*, n. 170 above; cf. Lord Steyn, "Does Legal Formalism Hold Sway in England?" (1996) 49 *Current Legal Problems* 43 at p. 46.

[171] R.L.Brown, "Activism is Not a Four-Letter Word" (2003) 73 *University of Colorado Law Review*. 1257.

law. Where else, one might ask, did the common law and the principles of equity come from, if it was not from judicial activity?

No one at the time described Chief Justice Coke's decision in *Dr Bonham's case*[172] as an instance of judicial activism. But that has certainly been a reaction to the assertion by Coke's contemporary counterpart, Lord Cooke of Thorndon, to the effect that there may be some rights in New Zealand that "lie so deep" that even Parliament cannot override them.[173] In the Australian context, because of our written Constitution, I have differed from Lord Cooke about this thesis both in[174] and out[175] of court. For my "conservatism" I have been criticised.[176] I would never dream of labelling Lord Cooke as a "judicial activist". But others, in so many words, have done so.[177]

It is written constitutions, with the politico-legal judgments that they inevitably demand, that have attracted the most furious assertions of judicial activism by those who have disagreed with particular rulings. When, in the early years of the Supreme Court of the United States, Chief Justice Marshall asserted the power of his court to declare an Act of Congress, or the conduct of federal officials, void (although such a power had not been expressly granted by the Constitution[178]) he and his Court were furiously attacked by President Jefferson. The justices of the Supreme Court were accused of subversion of the popular will.[179] It has been a recurring theme in constitutional adjudication ever since.

In the nineteenth and early twentieth centuries there were attacks of a similar kind upon conservative decisions of the

---

[172] *op. cit.*, n. 52 above.

[173] *Fraser v State Services Commission* [1984] 1 N.Z.L.R. 116 at 121; cf. P. Rishworth, "Lord Cooke and the Bill of Rights" in *The Struggle for Simplicity in the Law— Essays for Lord Cooke of Thorndon* (P. Rishworth ed., Butterworths, Wellington, 1997), p. 295, p. 298.

[174] *Building Construction Employees and Builders' Labourers Federation of NSW v Minister for Industrial Relations* (1986) 7 N.S.W.L.R. 372; *Durham Holdings Pty Ltd v New South Wales* (2001) 205 C.L.R. 399 at 419.

[175] Kirby, *op. cit.*, n. 53 above, at pp. 342–345.

[176] P.Lane, "Constitutional Implications and a Bill of Rights" (2001) 75 *Australian Law Journal* 469 at p. 470–471.

[177] J.Smillie, "Formalism, Fairness and Efficiency: Civil Adjudication in New Zealand" [1996] *New Zealand Law Review* 254 at p. 259–268; cf E.W.Thomas, "Judging in the 21st Century" [2000] *New Zealand Law Journal* 228 at p. 229; E.W.Thomas, "Fairness and Certainty in Adjudication: Formalism versus Substantialism" (1999) 9 *Otago Law Review* 459.

[178] *Marbury v Madison* 5 U.S. (1 Cranch) 137 (1803); cf. A. Lewis, Foreword to M. Kozlowski, *The Myth of the Imperial Judiciary* (N.Y.U. Press, New York, 2003), p. ix at ix.

[179] Justice, *op. cit.*, n. 41 above, at 302; cf. Lewis, *op. cit.*, n. 178 above, at ix.

Supreme Court.[180] In comparison, judges of the English tradition, at home and in most parts of Europe and the Commonwealth, were largely spared such venom. In part, the reason for
the comparative immunity from such calumny was that the role
of judges outside the United States was generally narrower.
Until recently few other judges enjoyed the large discretions of a
bill of rights. Most were protected from attack by the law of
contempt. Nearly all practised the "noble lie" of "strict and
complete legalism". In recent years, however, in Commonwealth countries (more than in the United Kingdom) attacks on
judges have become more frequent and increasingly less
restrained.

The United States probably still wins the prize for the most
egregious instances of excoriation of the judges. In the State
courts of that country the procedures of judicial election and
recall have encouraged the most extreme insults, epithets and
labels.[181] Candidates for election to the bench in the United
States promise to be "*too* tough on criminals".[182] Presidential
candidates consign named federal judges to the "judicial hall of
shame". They call for the impeachment of others.[183] One federal
judge of the District Court recently wrote of how his judicial
decisions, necessarily subject to appeal, have resulted in the
inclusion of his name on a "ten Most Wanted list" drawn up by
politicians.[184] He suggested that "judicial activism" has become:

> "more often than not a code word used to induce public disapproval
> of a court action that a politician opposes but is powerless to
> overturn. In most cases, the mindless incantation of the phrase
> amounts to a political retrial which touches the congregation of
> voters on an emotional level without promoting any reasoned
> discourse amongst them".[185]

[180] *e.g. Dred Scott v Sandford* 60 U.S. (19 How) 393 (1857) (constitutional legality of
slavery); *Plessy v Ferguson* 163 U.S. 537 (1896) (equal but separate racial
accommodation); *Lochner v New York* 198 U.S. 45 (1905) (constitutional inval-
idity of maximum wartime hours laws); *Korematsu v United States* 323 U.S. 214
(1944) (internment of Japanese Americans); *Dennis v United States* 341 U.S. 494
(1951) (validity of anti-communist laws).
[181] Some of these are collected in J. W. Bellacosa, "Remarks—Judging Cases v
Courting Public Opinion" (1997) 65 *Fordham Law Review* 2381.
[182] Reproduced in M.D.Kirby, "Attacks on Judges—A Universal Phenomenon"
(1998) 72 *Australian Law Journal* 599 at p. 602; S.B.Bright, "Political Attacks on
the Judiciary: Can Justice be Done Amidst Efforts to Intimidate or Remove
Judges from Office for Unpopular Decisions?" (1997) 72 *New York University
Law Review* 308 at p. 323.
[183] S.B.Bright, "Political Attacks on the Judiciary" (1997) 80 *Judicature* 165 at
p. 166.
[184] Justice, *op. cit.*, n 41 above, at p. 302.
[185] *ibid.*

Justice Ruth Bader Ginsburg of the United States Supreme Court has described the label of judicial activism as one "too often pressed into service by critics of court results rather than the legitimacy of court decisions".[186] Attacks on judges in this vein do not come only from the political right. Some of the recent "judge-bashing" in the United States has been targeted by the political left at the Supreme Court majority in *Bush v Gore*.[187] That decision effectively delivered the Presidency of the United States to Mr G. W. Bush. It did so by judicial decision rather than by the decision of Congress or the American people to whom federal statutes and the Constitution respectively appeared to assign the ultimate decision in cases of presidential elections.[188]

Because cases on the Bill of Rights tend to concern claims for legal protection of minorities, the powerless and the vulnerable, it is the judges who uphold such rights that tend to bring down on their heads the most vitriolic judge-bashing and name-calling. Some are denounced as "frenetically activist".[189] The attacks have become more vehement in recent years. Given the procedures for judicial confirmation, election and recall in the United States, in that country the result has been an attempt to bully the Bench. It has led to a reduction of extra-curricular judicial writing on law, judges doubtless hoping to deny partisan critics insights into their views.[190] It has produced tit-for-tat political responses in the United States Senate confirmation hearings, considering presidential nominations to judicial office. It stands as a warning of where the attacks on "judicial activism" can lead.

JUDICIAL "BASKET-WEAVERS"

Australians are also given to robust language. Strong epithets are often deployed to cut down so-called "tall poppies". In recent years political leaders and media pundits in Australia,

---

186 As quoted in D.H.Zeigler, "The New Activist Court" (1996) 45 *American University Law Review* 1367 at pp. 1367–1368.

187 531 U.S. 98 (2000).

188 Brooks, *op. cit.*, n. 105 above, at p. 46; cf. *Sue v Hill* (1999) 199 C.L.R. 462, *per* Kirby J., at 564–565.

189 Craven, *op. cit.*, n. 161 above, at p. 236.

190 S.S.Gaille, "Publishing by U.S. Court of Appeals Judges: Before and After the Bork Hearings" (1997) 26 *Journal of Legal Studies* 371.

together with a few local lawyers, have like naughty schoolboys jumped with gusto onto the "judicial activism" bandwagon. In 1998 I collected some of the more printable comments made by these critics concerning the then recent decisions of the High Court of Australia:

> "[T]he Court and the Justices were labelled 'bogus', 'pusillanimous and evasive', guilty of 'plunging Australia into the abyss', a 'pathetic . . . self-appointed [group of] Kings and Queens', a group of 'basket-weavers', purveyors of 'intellectual dishonesty', unaware of 'its place', 'adventurous', needing a 'good behaviour bond', needing, on the contrary, a sentence to 'life on the streets', an 'unfaithful servant of the Constitution', 'undermining democracy', a body 'packed with feral judges', 'a professional labor cartel' ".[191]

It was as if, having begun the invective and suffered no penalty, those involved felt encouraged to plumb still further depths. The traditional defender of the federal judiciary in Australia, the Federal Attorney-General, did not intervene to defend the judges or their courts. This was so, although he must have known that they could not do so effectively without damaging their offices. Instead, he maintained a Trappist-like silence.[192] He did so when I was attacked in the Federal Parliament, defending neither me nor my office.[193] In the warm after-glow of the centenary celebrations of the High Court of Australia in October 2003, it is as well to remember these things so that we do not become too starry-eyed but keep judicial feet firmly planted on the ground. Any judge of the common law today—including in the United Kingdom—who thinks that he or she is immune from this new tendency towards invective against judges had better think again.

Most of the decisions that attracted the charge of "judicial activism" in Australia were given before my appointment to the High Court. I do not feel personally defensive about them. I can look on them with reasonable dispassion. Four categories of cases are involved. It is instructive to examine them briefly for the lessons that they teach on this subject:

---

[191] Kirby, *op. cit.*, n. 182 above, at p. 601 (citations omitted).
[192] B.Heraghty, "Defender of the Faith? The Role of the Attorney-General in Defending the High Court" (2002) 28 *Monash University Law Review* 206.
[193] E.Campbell and M.Groves, "Attacks on Judges Under Parliamentary Privilege: A Sorry Australian Episode" [2002] *Public Law* 626. The article describes an attack on the author.

- In the first case, in *Dietrich v The Queen*,[194] the High Court reversed an earlier contrary ruling.[195] It held that an indigent person, facing trial for a serious offence, unable to afford a lawyer, was normally entitled to a stay of the trial until the state provided legal counsel to represent the accused in the trial. There are similar decisions elsewhere.[196] Given the established law on stays of seriously unjust proceedings and the great complexity of most modern criminal trials for unrepresented accused, the decision appears unsurprising.[197] That judges should ultimately decline to condone, or participate in, a charade of legal process is understandable, given their vocation. To grumble about this decision appears to evidence a degree of formalism that has temporarily forgotten what the central purpose of the legal and judicial system is. Yet grumblers and critics there are.

- A second case that raised tempers was *Mabo v Queensland [No 2]*.[198] That decision reversed a long understanding of the Australian common law to the effect that, at British settlement upon the acquisition of the radical title to land throughout Australia by the Crown at British settlement, all native title to land anywhere in the Australian continent had been extinguished. The decision upholding the survival of native title in Australia angered some farming, mining and legal interests. Yet one of the judges participating in the majority decision (Justice Michael McHugh) has recently declared that it was a comparatively simple case, resulting in a new legal conclusion when a fundamental factual premise of the old law was shown to have

---

[194] (1992) 177 C.L.R. 292; cf. L. Zines, "Judicial Activism and the Rule of Law in Australia" in *Judicial Power, Democracy and Legal Positivism* (T. Campbell and J. Goldsworthy eds., Aldershot, Ashgate, 2000) p. 391 at p. 393. The commentator G. Henderson called it a "political windfall for the recessed legal industry": "March of the High Court Murphyites" *Sydney Morning Herald*, February 1, 1992, at p. 13.

[195] *McInnis v The Queen* (1979) 143 C.L.R. 575.

[196] cf. *Powell v Alabama* 287 U.S. 45, *per* Sutherland J. (for the Court), at 68–69 (1932); *Gideon v Wainwright* 372 U.S. 335, *per* Black J. (for the Court), at 343–345 (1963).

[197] In the High Court of Australia, Brennan J. dissented on the ground that the decision was an unwarranted intrusion into legislative and executive functions. *Dietrich, op. cit.*, n. 194 above, at 322–323. Dawson J. dissented on the basis that an accused had no right to be represented at public expense: at 349–350.

[198] *op. cit.*, n. 34 above.

been false.[199] The decision in *Mabo* can be better understood in the context of similar decisions in other common law settler countries. In recent decades many such decisions have removed the flaws of past legal reasoning that could only be understood in terms of the attitudes of racial superiority. Today that consideration can surely have no place in the common law anywhere.[200] Yet grumblers and critics about *Mabo* remain.

- A third case that focused the attack on so-called judicial activism in Australia was one in which I participated: *Wik Peoples v Queensland*.[201] That decision held that the *Mabo* principle applied to pastoral leases over huge tracts of land comprising about 40 per cent of the Australian inland. The decision involved the application to the Australian statutes providing for pastoral leases of the well-established common law rule that basic civil rights are not taken to have been abolished by statute except by clear enactment. People—including Aboriginal people—do not lose important rights unless the law, depriving them of their claims, is very clear. If such a rule protects the legal privilege of wealthy corporations, its neutral application by a court of law could reasonably be demanded by indigenous people. According to Professor Leslie Zines, "the decision [in *Wik*] was fairly orthodox in its reasoning . . . [but] . . . fear and uncertainty was caused by some mischievous comments of Ministers who suggested that it was still uncertain whether Aboriginal title could be claimed on freehold land. As a result, word spread that suburban backyards were at risk".[202] Grumblers and critics never cease to complain about the *Wik* decision although they are silent about—and sometimes even participate in—the application of the same rule of statutory construction to protect others whom they perceive as more worthy—those more like themselves.

- A fourth group of Australian cases charged as instancing judicial activism, concerns decisions to uphold implications of free speech in the Australian Constitution, inferred by the High Court of Australia from the necessity

---

[199] *op. cit.*, n. 50 above, at 40–41. This was the belief that the indigenous people of Australia were wandering nomads with no effective connection to land.
[200] *op. cit.*, n. 34 above, *per* Brennan J., at 42.
[201] (1996) 187 C.L.R. 1.
[202] Zines, *op. cit.*, n. 194 above, p. 408.

to make the constitutional system of representative democracy effective and workable.[203] Another case of implied constitutional rights which upset some critics concerned the implication, found in the Constitution, that State courts, as potential receptacles of federal jurisdiction, had to enjoy basic freedom from legislative or governmental interference.[204] Of course, views may differ over the scope of such implications. However, deriving implications from written documents is rudimentary lawyering. In the high noon of "strict legalism" in Australian constitutional law, implications of great importance were derived by Justice Dixon and his colleagues, from the sparse constitutional text.[205] In more recent times, implications have been upheld, less justifiable in my view, to exempt some State judicial incomes from universal federal tax laws.[206] What the criticism of "judicial activism" therefore comes down to is not an objection to the idea or methodology of drawing implications from a written constitution. Instead, what the critics of supposed "activism" really object to are (as Justice Ginsburg noticed) the outcomes of particular cases. Their ire has been turned not on the judicial decisions and the reasons advanced to explain them but on the judges personally. Accusations of infidelity to duty and "judicial activism" have been hurled, sometimes by those who should have known better.

Normally, in the modern age, when error in a judicial outcome is alleged, the path of the common law, is appeal. In a final court, points can always be reargued in later cases. Critics can write their observations for the highest appellate court this side of heaven—the academic journals. Or they can say virtually anything they like on television, radio and in *op ed* columns in the newspapers. Nowadays, through the internet, they can, at

---

[203] *Theophanous v Herald and Weekly Times Ltd* (1994) 182 C.L.R. 104; *Australian Capital Television Pty Ltd v The Commonwealth* (1992) 177 C.L.R. 106. The implied free speech cases were reviewed and re-expressed in *Lange, op. cit.,* n. 155 above. See also *Australian Broadcasting Corporation v Lenah Game Meats Pty Ltd* (2002) 208 C.L.R. 199, *per* Kirby J., at 279; *per* Callinan J., at 298. See also *Roberts v Bass* (2002) 212 C.L.R. 1.

[204] *Kable, op. cit.,* n. 155 above.

[205] *e.g. Australian Communist Party, op. cit.,* n. 152 above; the *Boilermakers' Case, op. cit.,* n. 153 above; (1957) 95 C.L.R. 529 (PC). See Zines, *op. cit.,* n. 151 above, at pp. 13–14.

[206] *Austin, op. cit.,* n. 155 above.

virtually no cost, tell the entire world of their opinions. They can bombard email systems with their views, however intemperate and hare-brained they may be. Yet until now, in our legal tradition, it has not been usual to add personal insult and the questioning of judicial motives and integrity to the criticism. In many countries of the common law, that polite world is crumbling before our very eyes.

In Australia, following the *Wik* decision of the High Court, the Acting Prime Minister (Mr Tim Fischer), promised that the federal government would appoint "Capital C Conservative[s]" to replace future retiring Justices of the High Court.[207] His intervention earned him a reproof from Chief Justice Brennan.[208] It procured an apology. But that was all.

From this course of events, Professor Leslie Zines concluded that, in Australia, "the phrase 'judicial activism' [had] become common among certain politicians and commentators. One legal journalist described it simply as a 'swear word.'"[209] Although the High Court of Australia, like other final courts, had always been the subject of criticism, the calumny had become more personal and vituperative. It comes from both sides of the political spectrum.[210] Whatever its origin, "judge-bashing" is dangerous. It threatens public confidence in the independence of the judiciary. It weakens faith in the decisions of judges. Worst of all, it may drive judges and lawyers back to formalism, once again pulling over themselves the cloak of the pretence that disputed decisions are wholly value-free and that all present and future judicial decisions may be traced logically to past precedents and doctrine, without any input of policies and values. If that should happen, the gains of the legal Reformation

---

[207] See N.Savva, "Fischer seeks a more conservative court" *The Age* (Melbourne), March 5, 1997 at pp. 1–2. Appointments to the High Court of Australia since 1997 have been judged by observers by reference to this proclaimed criterion.

[208] Editorial, "Fischer sparks new High Court row" *The Age* (Melbourne), March 6, 1997 at p. 6; cf. Editorial, "Politicising High Court Appointments", *Courier Mail*, (Brisbane) March 10, 1997 at p. 10. For similar attacks in Canada see M. Plaxton, "The Formalist Conception of the Rule of Law and the *Marshall* Backlash" (2003) 8 *Review of Constitutional Studies* 66 referring to political and public reactions to *The Queen v Marshall* [1999] 3 S.C.R. 456, an indigenous fishing case.

[209] Zines, *op. cit.*, n. 194, at p. 408; cf. E. A. Young, "Judicial Activism and Conservative Politics" (2002) 73 *University of Colorado Law Review* 1139 at p. 1213.

[210] Handler, *op. cit.*, n. 112 above at p. 302; cf. Raskin, *op. cit.*, n. 117 above, at p. 242; J. Gava "Another Blast from the Past: Why the Left Should Embrace Strict Legalism" (2003) 27 *Melbourne University Law Review* 186.

will be lost. The judicial method will return to the cave of the Old Testament.[211]

GOSPEL OF THE COUNTER-REFORMATION

As in any intellectual movement, even one that is sometimes extreme and misguided, it may be accepted that the Counter-Reformationists draw strength from difficulties that can arise when judges, buoyed up by the legal Reformation, seek to explain their decisions by reference to principle and policy, not just the words of past legal authority.

I put to one side the contentions of some critics who claim that the legal Counter-Reformation is spearheaded by lawyers who indulge in an unnatural denial about the psychological processes of human reasoning and decision-making.[212] Such critics view such denials as an infantile regression unworthy even of serious consideration. I also set aside the analysis of political theorists and advocates of critical legal studies who portray the call for a return to Lord Reid's fairytale as the work of social and political conservatives "bolstering the structure of power that ensure[s] the containment of popular control over policy and politics so as to "reinforce the ideological domination of the power elite".[213] Opinions like these are strongly held. But they by no means tell the full story.

It is important to notice some of the more thoughtful arguments that the Counter-Reformationists have deployed in this debate. Occasionally they make good points. Indeed, I will use these in my next lecture to shape a resolution that secures the gains that we have made in the legal Reformation without surrendering those gains to a resurgence of legal formalism.

For a lawyer raised under a written constitution, which envisages the judiciary as a branch of government kept separate from the legislature and Executive, the starting point for analysis

---

[211] F.Carrigan, "A Blast from the Past: The Resurgence of Legal Formalism" (2003) 27 *Melbourne University Law Review* 163 at p. 164. The author refers to recent writings of members of the High Court of Australia appointed since 1996 and to Smillie, *op. cit.*, n. 177 above; J. L. Pierce, "Interviewing Australia's Senior Judiciary" (2002) 37 *Australian Journal of Political Science* 131 at p. 135.

[212] Raskin, *op. cit.*, n. 117 above, at p. 242.

[213] Carrigan, *op. cit.*, n. 211 above, at pp. 181–185; Young, *op. cit.*, n. 209 above, at p. 1140; cf. Smillie, *op. cit.*, n. 177 above, at p. 256; S. B. Presser, "What A Real Conservative Believes About 'Judicial Ideology'" (2003) 2d: 6 *The Green Bag* 285 at p. 287.

is the principle that the separation of powers reflects the fact that the judiciary does not enjoy the entitlements in law-making that belong to the principal lawmakers in the Legislature and the Executive.[214] This basic point constitutes a salutary and constitutional reminder of an important judicial principle. Yet it is one that cannot be pressed to extremes. In discharging their functions, judges in a common law country, have always enjoyed a quasi-legislative role. As Cardozo put it:

> "The power to declare the law contains the power, and within limits, the duty, to make the law".[215]

It is not a breach of the separation of powers doctrine for a court, in expounding the common law, interpreting a statute or construing a written constitution, to discharge this traditional but limited role of lawmaking. Nevertheless, the separation of powers principle reminds judges that there is a necessary boundary. Judges must not cross it if they are to adhere to their proper function. If they go too far they risk damaging the source of their independence and authority.[216] To those brought up with the doctrine of parliamentary supremacy, as lawyers in the United Kingdom have been, it is not perhaps so necessary to be reminded of the need for deference as it is for those who enjoy the constitutional power of invalidation of statutes.[217] That great power has such large ramifications that it necessarily contains within itself the pressure to limit its use.

There are connected points that go beyond constitutional theory. They too act as a break on legitimate judicial rule-making. In our form of society, an elected legislature (or Executive whether separately elected or answerable to the legislature) has both the moral and legal responsibility for making most substantial changes in the law.[218] To the extent that judges assume that responsibility, where it should, and would, have been performed by elected officials, such judges diminish the democratic elements in lawmaking.[219] However imperfect

---

[214] *Stringer v Government of the Philippine Islands* 277 U.S. 189, *per* Sutherland J. (for the Court) at 201 (1928); cf. *Boilermakers' Case, op. cit.,* n. 205 above, *per curiam,* at 541 (PC).

[215] Cardozo, *op. cit.,* n 168 above, p. 123, discussed in Walker, *op. cit.,* n. 110 above, p. 211.

[216] Lord Scarman cited by Lord Bingham, *op. cit.,* n. 115 above, p. 5.

[217] Walker, *op. cit.,* n. 110 above, p. 237.

[218] A point made in *Mabo, op. cit.,* n. 34 above, *per* Dawson J. (diss.), at 175; cf. Young, *op. cit.,* n. 209 above, at p. 1245.

[219] J.Gava, "The Rise of the Hero Judge" (2001) 24 *University of New South Wales Law Journal* 747 at p. 748. See also *United States v Marshall* 908 F 2d 1312, *per* Posner J. (diss.), at 1335 (7th Circuit, 1990).

elected government may sometimes appear, the principle oblig-
ing the people to take the ultimate responsibility for matters
affecting themselves, and not to leave difficult decisions to an
elite of "experts", is one that constitutions enshrine and that
human rights instruments uphold.[220] "Experts" may have insufficient empathy, or experience, to determine the most acceptable
and suitable shape of the law. At least, this may be so where
large questions of policy are involved.[221]

As a general rule, in an age when the effectiveness of
democratic institutions is being attacked on many fronts, we
should generally be striving to enhance rather than to diminish
accountable lawmaking.[222] In proper cases, this will mean judges
deferring to law making by the elected representatives of the
people.[223]

Many elected officials will have had a much wider range of
human experience than the average judge.[224] The vulnerability
of political representatives to dismissal from office, or recall,
may increase their resistance to unreasonable, excessive or over-
reaching lawmaking.[225] Elected personnel may have a greater
tendency to compromise than do those who follow logic where
it leads.[226] They may be more easily able to initiate or to conduct
enquiries, the collection of data and the gathering of expert
opinions antecedent to good law-making. A judge, on the other
hand, will usually be limited by the conduct of a case by others.
The judge will largely be restricted to the issues that the parties
argue. The techniques inherent in judicial adjudication are more
confining than those available to the other branches of government when those branches turn their attention to law-making.[227]

Further, the outcome of adjudication is virtually always
disappointing and costly to losers. Especially if (on the basis of
past understandings of the law) they had reason to assume that

---

[220] *e.g. International Covenant on Civil and Political Rights,* art. 25.
[221] *South Australia v The Commonwealth* (1942) 65 C.L.R. 373, *per* Latham C.J., at
408–409; cf. Campbell, *op. cit.,* n. 5 above, at p. 313–314; Craven, *op. cit.,* n. 160
above, at p. 234.
[222] T.I.Lowi, Review (1985) 63 *Texas Law Review* 1591 at p. 1593; Scalia, *op. cit.,*
n. 161 above, p. 24.
[223] *Libman v Attorney-General Quebec* (1997) 151 D.L.R. (4th) 385; cf. M. Zander, *The
State of Justice* (51st Hamlyn lectures, 1999) (Sweet & Maxwell, London, 2000),
p. 84.
[224] Heydon, *op. cit.,* above, n. 37, at p. 124–125; cf. Gleeson, *op. cit.,* above, n. 144 at
p. 9.
[225] Campbell, *op. cit.,* n. 5 above, at pp. 313–315.
[226] *Australian Conservation Foundation v The Commonwealth* (1980) 146 C.L.R. 493,
per Gibbs J., at p. 529.
[227] Parkinson, *op. cit.,* n. 13 above, at p. 186.

their view of the law would prevail, a sudden redefinition of the applicable rules may leave the disappointed parties with a complaint that their reliable expectations have been frustrated.[228] The inability of most common law courts to fashion orders limited to prospective effect,[229] and the potential of judicial decisions to have a retrospective operation on the parties and many others in society,[230] can sometime afford reasons for withholding a judicial change in the law even where defects of the law have been clearly proved.[231] Respect for other law-makers and a sense of modesty about the judges' power to know, and to evaluate, all relevant considerations when re-expressing a rule of law are further reasons for keeping judicial creativity in check.[232]

As a practical matter, adhering to judicial restraint also tends to fend off the "political firestorms" which controversial restatements of the law are likely to whip up. The attacks on the judiciary, in many lands in recent years may, in some cases, have encouraged a return to the ideology of formalism.[233] It may have increased the historical doubts about judicial capacity to improve the law,[234] particularly in areas where earlier legal authority is relatively clear.[235]

Like every appellate judge, I have, from time to time, heeded such admonitions of restraint. For example, I did so in a case envisaging an increase of landlord liability in negligence which I saw as having large and unknowable economic potential.[236] I did so in another case involving the suggested enlargement of

---

[228] *Cassell and Co Ltd v Broome* [1972] A.C. 1027, *per* Lord Hailsham, at 1054; cf. Bennion, *op. cit.*, n. 52 above, at p. 685 citing *Black-Clawson International Ltd v Papierwerke Waldhof-Aschaffenberg AG* [1975] A.C. 591, *per* Lord Diplock, at 638.

[229] *Ha v New South Wales* (1997) 189 C.L.R. 465, *per* Brennan C.J., McHugh, Gummow and Kirby J.J., at 503–504. But see *McKinney v The Queen* (1991) 171 C.L.R. 468, *per* Mason C.J., Deane, Gaudron and McHugh J.J. at 478 where a new "rule of practice" in relation to uncorroborated police interrogation was announced for the future.

[230] Heydon, *op. cit.*, n. 37 above, at pp. 14–15; cf. *Eastern Associated Coal Corp. v United Mine Workers of America, District 17* 531 U.S. 57 (2000), *per* Scalia J. (diss.), at 69.

[231] S.Taylor Jr., "The Last True Believer in Judicial Restraint" *The Atlantic Online*, April 23, 2002.

[232] Pierce, *op. cit.*, n. 211 above, at p. 140.

[233] *ibid.*, at p. 135.

[234] Walker, *op. cit.*, n. 110 above, at p. 216.

[235] Smillie, *op. cit.*, n. 177 above, at p. 256.

[236] *Northern Sandblasting Pty Ltd v Harris* (1997) 188 C.L.R. 313 at 398; cf. H. Stowe, "'The Unruly Horse' Has Bolted: *Tinsley v Milligan*" (1994) 57 *Modern Law Review* 441 at p. 444 referring to *Tinsley v Milligan* [1993] 3 All E.R. 65, *per* Lord Goff, at 79.

criminal liability beyond that provided by a recent enactment.[237] I did so in a case involving defamation on the internet, where a completely new legal regime was proposed by a party which made some very powerful criticisms of the established law when applied to such a radically new medium.[238] I did so in the case of liability for the costs of upbringing a child born following negligent advice about an incomplete sterilisation operation.[239]

In the last-mentioned decision, the application of the settled common law principles of recovery for negligence favoured the plaintiff. To cut damages off arbitrarily, awarding a fixed or "conventional" sum, involved "activism" which, I thought, was a matter for Parliament, not for the courts. In Australia, legislatures have not hesitated to enact caps and limitations on recovery or to provide specified zones of immunity from liability in tort. On one view, legislators and not the judges should wear the accountability for doing this. However, media and political pundits, commenting on the case, portrayed the Court majority's adherence to the common law principle as "judicial activism".[240] In fact, it was exactly the opposite. Truly, the decision represented a case of judicial restraint and the principled application of settled law. Perhaps this only goes to prove that "judicial activism" exists in the eye of the beholder.[241] It is a phrase used to wound and curse its object rather than to invite a reasoned debate.

Many arguments are advanced to oppose reliance on policy considerations in reaching judicial conclusions. Typically, such modes of reasoning are castigated as the purest form of "judicial activism". One argument concerns the difficulty that judges will often face in evaluating community attitudes and needs beyond the judge's own moral convictions, assessment and experience.[242] Another is the special inhibition about altering the longstanding authority of the common law. Done too often, this could import a sense of uncertainty about the law and its institutions.[243] Another reason for judicial inaction is the risk of

---

[237] *Lipohar v The Queen* (1999) 200 C.L.R. 485 at 563.

[238] *Dow Jones and Co Inc v Gutnick* (2002) 210 C.L.R. 575. cf. *Trigwell, op. cit.*, n. 30 above, *per* Mason J., at 633–634; *per* Murphy J. (diss.), at 652–653.

[239] *Cattanach, op. cit.*, n. 94 above, 77 A.L.J.R. 1312 at 1348; 199 A.L.R. 131 at 180.

[240] It was criticised in the media by the Prime Minister, attacked by the Deputy Prime Minister and denounced by the usual media suspects.

[241] *Justice, op. cit.*, n. 41 above, p. 304.

[242] *Smillie, op. cit.*, n. 177 above, p. 261.

[243] J.Kelly and M.Murphy, "Confronting Judicial Supremacy: A Defence of Judicial Activism and the Supreme Court of Canada's Legal Rights Jurisprudence" (2001) 16 *Canadian Journal of Law and Society* 3, at pp. 8–12.

inconsistency in judicial outcomes, when the decision on restraint or re-expression of the law turns on a judge's conclusion that a particular result would be "intolerable". As Justice Holmes once put it, what is intolerable is what "makes me puke".[244] This is a somewhat unstable and highly personal criterion.

Judges may accept that those who originally expressed the rules of the common law (or the previously settled interpretation of a statute or written constitution) may have done so from the standpoint of the knowledge and values which they then had. However, critics find the uncertainty of the criteria for change in legal authority intolerably threatening to their ideology of certain law and a completely dispassionate and neutral judiciary.[245] They attack consideration of issues that venture wider than attention to the words of the texts governing the exact matter in contest.[246] They contend that going further has a greater potential to undermine judicial legitimacy than attacks on individual judges will do.[247] For such critics, it is the activists that subvert the rule of law, not those who by their criticisms try to hold the line.[248]

THE COUNTER-REFORMATION AND HUMAN RIGHTS

The introduction of the discourse about legally enforceable rights into the common law system, previously resistant to such an approach, has historically grown, as Lord Scarman pointed out, largely in consequence of the work of Anglo-American lawyers on the post-Second World War statements of universal human rights. In her Hamlyn Lectures in 1990, Claire Palley[249] traced the advance of this development to Lord Scarman's own Hamlyn lectures twenty years earlier.[250]

[244] Holmes, cited R.A.Posner, *Overcoming Law* (Harvard University Press, Cambridge Mass., 1995), 192. On the suggested inconsistency of United States constitutional decision-making see *e.g. Lawrence, op. cit.*, n. 162 above, (homosexual rights) and Kozinski J. in *Silveira v Lockyer* 328 F.3d 567 (2003) (right to bear arms). For criticism of the majority opinion in *Bush v Gore* see Young, *op. cit.*, n. 209 above, p. 1156.

[245] C.Howard, "The High Court" (1994) 4 *Proceedings of the Samuel Griffith Society* 65 at p. 67.

[246] Heydon, *op. cit.*, n. 37 above, pp. 120–121.

[247] H.Patapan, "High Court Review, 2001: Politics, Legalism and the Gleeson Court" (2002) 37:2 *Australian Journal of Political Science* 241.

[248] Campbell, *op. cit.*, n. 5 above, p. 326.

[249] C Palley, *The United Kingdom and Human Rights* (43rd Hamlyn Lectures, 1990) (Sweet & Maxwell, London, 1991), p. 123.

[250] Lord Scarman, *English Law—The New Dimension* (26th Hamlyn Lectures, 1974) (Stevens, London, 1974). See also Zander, *op. cit.*, n. 223 above, p. 77.

In most common law countries the challenge of marrying the new law of human rights with the old law must be accepted by courts although the enthusiasm for engaging judges in human rights decisions is by no means universal.[251] In his Reith Lectures in 1987, Lord McCluskey lamented that human rights law had turned judges into legislators. He complained that such a power made the mistake of "dressing up policy choices as if they were legal choices".[252]

In Australia, we have so far remained a citadel of resistance to a constitutional bill of rights.[253] However, in the United Kingdom (and virtually everywhere else) a new era of human rights law has dawned. According to Lord Steyn, in interpreting and applying a charter of rights, "the straight-jacket of legal logic is not enough".[254] So much may be accepted. But what is to be put in its place?

In countries that have become used to the application of fundamental human rights law, it is often difficult for observers to imagine a legal system without such a means for protecting minorities, the weak and the powerless against majoritarian democracy, and doing so in legal proceedings decided by judges. But in countries, like New Zealand, South Africa and the United Kingdom, where such laws have only recently been adopted, there are bound to be tensions as some judges and lawyers resent, and resist, the "politicisation of legal decision-making"[255] and as others embark upon the task with energy and decisiveness. Many of those in the vanguard of the legal Counter-Reformation are deeply hostile to notions of fundamental human rights. Ironically, despite the texts and all the legal developments that have occurred, they want to return to, or stay in, a world in which such rights are kept in check and judges stay as far away from them as possible.

In Australia, the slightest introduction of "rights talk"[256] has a tendency to make the leaders of the legal Counter-Reformation

---

[251] See *e.g.* Lord McCluskey, *Law, Justice and Democracy* (Reith Lectures, 1987) (British Broadcasting Corporation, London, 1987) cited in Zander, *op. cit.*, n. 223 above, p. 79.

[252] Lord McCluskey, *ibid.*, p. 34.

[253] Nevertheless, the jurisprudence of international human rights appears in different forms as an influence on the development of the common law (*Mabo, op. cit.*, n. 34 above, *per* Brennan J., at 42) and, in my view, of constitutional interpretation (*Kartinyeri v The Commonwealth* (1998) 195 C.L.R. 337, *per* Kirby J., at 417–419).

[254] Lord Steyn, *op. cit.*, n. 166 above, at p. 19.

[255] A.Ashworth, *Human Rights, Serious Crime and Criminal Procedure* (54th Hamlyn lectures, 2001) (Sweet & Maxwell, London, 2002), p. 87.

[256] Patapan, *op. cit.*, n. 247 above, p. 251.

apoplectic. They see proposals for a constitutional charter of rights as a frontal attack on their notion of the rule of law and of a legitimate judicial method.[257] As for the introduction of the principles of human rights by the techniques of common law elaboration, these are denounced as a Trojan horse.[258] They are viewed as an activist importation of unincorporated treaties "by the back door".[259]

The advocates of the Counter-Reformation quake in their shoes at the thought of "hero judges" released to "strut their stuff".[260] It is too late, in their view, to save the United Kingdom from this foreign folly. But in the South Seas lies a big land which they hope will keep the flame of the true faith of the common law judge alive until the rest of the world repents the error of its present ways.[261]

I used to share some of these views. Fortunately, I grew out of the spell of formalism and its fairytales. In my final lecture, I will present a Concordat. Out of a marriage of the truths won by the legal Reformation and the legitimate points presented by the more thoughtful advocates of the Counter-Reformation, wisdom and a middle way may be found. We need a middle ground that is typical of the common law and the pragmatic approach it usually adopts. The extremes of unbounded judicial creativity and invention will be tamed. But the call for a return to the verbal formalism of past judicial reasoning and for "strict and complete legalism" will be rejected as the fairy tale that the legal Reformation taught it was.

---

[257] Craven, *op. cit.*, n. 161 above; cf. Kelly and Murphy, *op. cit.*, n. 243 above, p. 7.
[258] Heydon, *op. cit.*, n. 37 above, at p. 131, a reference to my decision in *Young v Registrar*, Court of Appeal (No 3), (1993) 32 N.S.W.L.R. 262 at 276.
[259] cf. *Teoh*, *op. cit.*, n. 34 above, *per* Mason and Deane J.J., at 288.
[260] Gava, *op. cit.*, n. 219 above, pp. 757–758.
[261] Davies, *op. cit.*, n. 21 above, p. 37.

4. Concordat

IN SEARCH OF COMMON GROUND

I began these lectures with a description of the Old Testament of the judicial method. It was a tale of formalism that embraced the "noble lie" that judges merely declared, and did not make, the law. In the twentieth century the realists and truth-tellers dispelled this fictitious world in a great legal Reformation that described the judicial method as it was: not the romantic dream of the fictitious past that portrayed the judicial function as nothing more than the product of "strict logic and high technique".

In my third lecture I described the way in which a legal Counter-Reformation has begun to spread in the countries of the common law: involving perennial attacks on judges for candidly identifying the considerations of policy that had influenced the choices they made in their decisions and for seeking to remove anomalies, inconsistencies and serious injustices from the law. Such judges are assailed by powerful voices in politics, business, the media and elsewhere as "judicial activists". They are accused of naked usurpation of the lawmaking power.[262] As purveyors of "judicial wilfulness".[263] As "subverters of the principles of the Constitution".[264] As "hero judges",[265] hell-bent on personal power, antagonistic to democratic law-making.[266] If they could not stick to the *application* of the law but insist on

---

[262] Parkinson, *op. cit.*, n. 13 above, p. 195.
[263] *e.g. Voinovich v Women's Medical Professional Corp.* 523 U.S. 1036, *per* Thomas J. (diss.), at 1039 (1998); cf. Lasser, *op. cit.*, n. 59 above, at 882.
[264] Gleeson, *op. cit.*, n. 143 above, at p. 11 citing *The Global Expansion of Judicial Power* (C.N.Tate and T.Vallinder eds., N.Y.U. Press, New York, 1995).
[265] Gava, *op. cit.*, n. 219 above, p. 752.
[266] Young, *op. cit.*, n. 209 above, at p. 1145 referring to A.Bickel, *The Least Dangerous Branch: The Supreme Court at the Bar of Politics* (2nd ed., Yale University Press, New Haven, 1986), p. 146.

making it their duty, so it is said, is clear. They should resign.[267]
There is no place on the Bench for their infidelity to law.[268]

The most vehement examples of the Counter-Reformation may be found in the United States and Australia. But there is evidence that a similar movement may be getting underway in the United Kingdom. In 1995 the Home Secretary, Mr Michael Howard, launched a series of vitriolic attacks on the judiciary. Following one case, in which Justice Dyson in the High Court ruled that the Home Secretary had acted unlawfully in respect of prisoner appeals, Mr Howard declared: "The last time this particular judge found against me . . . the Court of Appeal unanimously decided that he was wrong". Ten years earlier, such a statement would not have been made by a Minister of the Crown.

In more recent times, the present Home Secretary, Mr David Blunkett, has attacked judges in similar terms for performing their functions of judicial review of administrative decisions.[269] His attacks provoked Lord Alexander of Weedon Q.C. to declare that the Minister was: "Deeply antagonistic to the judiciary and to the legal profession when his ministerial wishes are thwarted".

As the functions of the courts in judicial review, and in the application of the Human Rights Act 1998 (UK), are enlarged, and as new functions to invalidate laws and administrative actions are imposed on the judiciary by the *European Constitution* should it come into effect, judges and lawyers in the United Kingdom must get ready. If the American, Australian and Canadian experience is any guide, the full force of the legal Counter-Reformation will not be far away from Britain.

Some of that force will, as I have shown, draw upon legitimate concerns about theory and practice, occasionally enlivened by particular judicial decisions. But it will also arise from a highly conservative group in the law, in politics and other places of power who want to restore the previous doctrine about judicial decisions. Such critics of the legal Reformation are indifferent, or blind, to its enlightenment. Some are deeply antagonistic to the candid recognition of the fact that judges are not, and should not be, automatons: blindly applying law unchanged and exactly as derived from the past.

[267] A.M.Gleeson, *The Rule of Law and the Constitution* (Boyer Lectures 2000) (Australian Broadcasting Commission, Sydney 2000), p. 127.

[268] Gleeson, *op. cit.*, n. 144 above, at p. 11.

[269] F.Gibb, "Blunkett v The Bench: The Battle has Begun", *The Times Online*, March 4, 2003.

Unless lawyers of the present age are alert to the Counter-Reformation, it is likely that we will end up with disgraceful incidents of judicial witch-hunting such as have occurred in the United States. We will witness the bullying of judges in an endeavour to force them to draw back from honesty in the discharge of their functions so as to avoid threatened political heat from those who prefer an inert judiciary: one that denies its legitimate creative role.[270]

When the agitprop of the rhetoric of the Counter-Reformation is stripped away, there remain some valid ideas which the less polemical opponents of realism and transparency in judicial reasoning have expressed. Somewhere between the spectre of a lawless judge, pursuing political ideas of his or her own from the judicial seat, irrespective of the law, and the idealised mechanic of the daydreams of the strict formalists, lies a place in which real judges perform their duties: neither wholly mechanical nor excessively creative.

I have called this last lecture "Concordat". Behind the polemics of the advocates of the legal Reformation and Counter-Reformation, there is a common ground. Identifying that common ground and reflecting upon its contours may conjure up a vision of the contemporary judiciary that is at once alert to some of the pitfalls argued by the ideology of the Counter-Reformation and at the same time a judiciary that adheres to the path of truth and self-knowledge which the realists introduced in the enlightenment of the legal Reformation.

By using the terminology of a papal treaty of peace for this last lecture, I do not suggest the ultimate ascendancy of the legal Counter-Reformation. On the contrary, it is my view that the Reformation, being grounded in truth and rationality about the judicial role, will henceforth remain the dominant model for the judicial method in common law countries. But any movement for change, in politics, religion and law, can occasionally go too far. It is, therefore, timely to explore the area of concurrence over the judicial method to which the present age has brought us.

AN ELUSIVE BOUNDARY

It is difficult to identify satisfactorily the criteria by which the contemporary common law judge can legitimately exercise the

---

[270] Walker, *op. cit.*, n. 110 above; Pierce, *op. cit.*, n. 211 above, at p. 135.

judicial power in a given case to express, or to decline to express, a new rule of law or to state an existing rule in new and different terms.

Some authors have returned empty-handed from the quest to find such criteria.[271] Lord Reid, in the same essay in which he denounced the "fairytale" of formalism, explained why the search for an objective criterion to distinguish the case for creativity from the case for restraint was bound to be elusive. He said that it was because people want fundamentally inconsistent things from the law. They want it to be certain and predictable (considerations promoting restraint). But they also want it to be just and therefore capable of moving with the times (considerations favouring creativity).[272] Lord Goff of Chieveley admitted that he was never quite sure where to locate the boundary between legitimate judicial development of the law and refusal of the task in a particular case in favour of parliamentary legislation.[273] Similar difficulties have been acknowledged by Australian writers.[274] Some of them have suggested the need for a comprehensive theory or approach.[275]§ They have accepted the legitimacy of the demand for an identification of the criteria by which the choice is ultimately to be made. Others are more dubious about the search for objectivity in such things.

Patrick Atiyah, in his Hamlyn Lectures, acknowledged the opinions of those who denied the possibility of formulating any comprehensive theory of judicial creativity.[276] Yet he was not convinced that this was so. Indeed, he pointed out that, once the declaratory theory of the judicial function was abandoned and a creative role of judicial legislation frankly admitted, it was imperative to mark out the legitimate frontier of that role. Only then would all lawmakers be aware of the boundaries of their respective constitutional functions.[277]

Without a theory of the permissible limits of the judge in lawmaking, it is difficult to have a serious debate about judicial activism and restraint, except in terms of visceral reactions to particular judicial outcomes. Angry demands that judges should

---

[271] Winfield, *op. cit.*, n. 83 above, p. 100.

[272] *cf.* Lord Reid, *op. cit.*, n. 169 above, p. 26.

[273] *Woolwich Equitable Building Society v Commissioners of Inland Revenue* [1993] A.C.70, *per* Lord Goff, at 173.

[274] Sackville, *op. cit.*, n. 41 above, at p. 67; Doyle, *op. cit.*, n. 7 above, p. 92.

[275] Horrigan, *op. cit.*, n. 111 above, p. 38.

[276] Atiyah, *op. cit.*, n. 80 above, p. 159 citing N.MacCormick, *Legal Reasoning and Legal Theory* (O.U.P., Oxford, 1978), p. 128.

[277] Atiyah, *ibid.*, pp. 159–163.

not "make" but merely "apply" the law are answered with the question: "But what is the law?" "How can it be expressed without a human mediator who is bound to state the applicable ideas in words that are all too often ambiguous or uncertain, thereby necessitating a process of choice"?

A CONSTITUTIONAL THEORY

In every society rules of law, to be binding, must enjoy validity from a constitutional source. In most countries, like my own, that source is a written document, perhaps supplemented by other important written instruments. In the United Kingdom, the sources of constitutional law are more numerous and complex. But formal requirements for the identification of rules that are binding as law there must be.

In the case of the rules of the common law, they will exist in the pronouncements made by superior courts in the past in terms necessary to support judicial orders binding on parties. In the space left by gaps between the legal rules stated in constitutional documents, statutes and valid laws made under them, a rule stated in the particular case may become a precedent to be applied by subordinate and co-equal courts in cases presenting the same or a like problem.

In a naïve approach to the constitutional separation of powers, it is sometimes said that judges should avoid lawmaking altogether, leaving it to Parliament because of the democratic legitimacy of a legislature which unelected judges can never enjoy. Whilst there is a grain of truth in this theory of the constitution,[278] its logic cannot be pressed too far. In reality, in parliaments created after the Westminster model, the legislators are often, in fact, subordinate to the power of the Executive once they elect it. In our complex society the Executive, in turn, is often heavily dependant upon unelected officials. The judiciary plays its mediating role. This includes the expression of new rules of the common law for new circumstances left open by gaps in the written law.

It is beyond contest that some of the accretions of power to the judiciary over the last century have come about as a result of failures and inadequacies in lawmaking by the other branches and departments of government.[279] Constitutional power hates a

---

[278] *Durham Holdings Pty Ltd v New South Wales* (2001) 205 C.L.R. 399, *per* Kirby J., at 429; *Building Construction Employees, op. cit.,* n. 174 above, *per* Kirby P, at pp. 404–405.

[279] Kirby, *op. cit.,* n. 53 above, at p. 353; Kirby, *op. cit.,* n. 68 above, at p. 1794.

vacuum. Where it exists, in the form of silence, confusion or uncertainty about the law, it is natural that those affected, despairing of solutions from the other law-making organs of government, will sometimes approach the judicial branch for what is in effect a new rule. They will seek a new law that responds quickly to their particular problem. When this happens judges, if they have jurisdiction in the case, are not normally at liberty to just send the parties away. How do they decide whether the fulfilment of their judicial role permits, or requires, the giving of an answer or obliges them to decline and force the parties to return to the politicians or bureaucrats? To what extent must judges defer to Parliament, when they know full well, from many like cases, that nothing will be done because the problem is too particular, divisive, technical or boring to merit political attention and parliamentary time? What, in other words, is the judicial role in the particular case?[280]

FIRST IDENTIFY LEGAL AUTHORITY

Subject to any constitutional restrictions, a legislature can normally do what it likes in making the law. But a judge has no such freedom. A judge must operate within a complex world of rules, mostly made by others. The judicial function is therefore always tethered to a rule or principle of law.

Sometimes the law may be clear, binding and immediately applicable. Sometimes it may be obscure and at best discovered by analogical reasoning applied to a decision in a case. Sometimes it will bear only remote similarities to earlier cases or texts propounded to solve the problem. But, ultimately, in the common law system, there is never a gap in the law. Gaps are filled by the constitution and other written laws and the rules and principles derived by the judges from earlier decisions. Discovering the applicable norm, explaining and applying it, is an intellectual not a polemical task.[281] But it is a task that commonly requires selection amongst competing choices.

Because there is now such a huge body of written and unwritten law, the scope for freedom of judicial action is in some senses narrower than it was in earlier times.[282] On the

---

[280] A.Barak, "A Judge on Judging: The Role of a Supreme Court in a Democracy" (2002) 116 *Harvard Law Review* 16 at p. 19.

[281] K.M.Hayne, "Letting Justice be Done without the Heavens Falling" (2001) 27 *Monash University Law Review* 12 at p. 18.

[282] Winfield, *op. cit.*, n. 83 above, p. 99; Hayne, *ibid.*, at p. 17.

other hand, the grafting onto common law systems of the notions of fundamental human rights has introduced a new, and legitimate, stimulus to creativity in judicial lawmaking. At least it has done so in those countries that have their own binding human rights charters or that permit regard to be had in judicial law-making to global or regional statements of fundamental rights.

The common law is hierarchical. Judicial officers lower in the hierarchy of courts are generally more constrained by their duties of obedience to binding authority. Their susceptibility to appeal and judicial review and the self-image of their function and pressures of work reinforce such constraints.[283] On the other hand, a final court of appeal[284] (and to a lesser extent other appellate courts[285]) enjoy a larger role in stating and refining the law in ways that sometimes give rise to a greater creativity.

It is generally in final courts that landmark cases are decided. *Donoghue v Stevenson*,[286] on negligence in the House of Lords is probably the best known case of the twentieth century. The *Mabo case*[287] on native title rights, in the High Court of Australia, is an Australian equivalent. Usually, as in such cases, an issue about the content of a fundamental principle of the common law has been bubbling away for years, even decades, before an appeal, with suitable facts, arrives in the final court. Once it does arrive, it may then elicit a new and significant decision of legal principle.

Often, as in such cases, there will be strong dissenting opinions on the part of judges who resist the re-configuration of the law favoured by the majority. Typically, the dissenting judges will urge, as all of us have sometimes done, adherence to the old rules. Every country of the common law (and doubtless others besides) can boast of such great cases.[288] Sometimes, as in the *Dred Scott* case,[289] affirming the lawfulness of slavery under

---

[283] Callinan, *op. cit.*, n. 124 above, at p. 98; Gleeson, *op. cit.*, n. 143 above, p. 10. However, it can also, in sharply partisan situations, it can also enlarge the attacks by judges on each other as has occurred in the United States Court of Appeals for the 6th Circuit: C.Lane, "Republicans Investigate Judge in Michigan Case" *Washington Post*, November 1, 2003, A1.

[284] *Garcia v National Australia Bank Limited* (1998) 194 C.L.R. 395, *per* Gaudron, McHugh, Gummow and Hayne J.J., at 403.

[285] *Nguyen v Nguyen* (1990) 169 C.L.R. 245, *per* Dawson, Toohey and McHugh J.J., at 268–270.

[286] *op. cit.*, n. 9 above, *per* Lord Atkin, at 580; cf. Doyle, *op. cit.*, n. 7 above, at p. 96.

[287] *op. cit.*, n. 34 above.

[288] See E.O'Dell (ed.), *Leading Cases of the Twentieth Century* (Round Hall, London, 2000).

[289] *op. cit.*, n. 180 above.

the United States Constitution, such decisions have had pro-
foundly adverse outcomes. *Dred Scott*, for example, may have
contributed to the outbreak of the Civil War in the United
States.[290] Usually, however, because of the pragmatic wisdom of
the judges, the results of such cases are quickly absorbed. Before
too long, where they have involved a major change, they are
accepted as settled and as beneficial.

A final court in a common law country has an inescapable
responsibility to filter the myriad of cases decided earlier and
below and to check the rules emerging from those cases against
the fundamental principles and purposes of the law. The judges
must do this viewing law not as an end in itself but as a means
contributing to a just and ordered society.[291] In this sense,
looking at law functionally, a final court has to act as a kind of
barometer—a recurrent reality check—on the way the legal
system is operating. Far from being a role antithetical to the
duty of judges, this is precisely how the hierarchical system of
the common law is supposed to work. Far from being a threat or
challenge to the superior lawmaking power of the legislature,
this is the fulfilment of the interstitial lawmaking function of the
courts in every land of the common law.[292] In most matters—
and in some countries in virtually all matters—a legislature that
does not like what the courts have done, can step in and re-
fashion the law to its own liking. The catalyst for action may be
a judge's decision.

OCCASIONS OF RESTRAINT

It would be foolish to deny that complex factors affect the
inclination of judges, either generally or on particular occasions,
to respond to a call for a novel legal approach or to opt for
restraint when invited to restate an old rule or make a new one.
Scaleograms, with their analysis of judicial voting patterns in the
United States, Australia and Britain[293] describe the generally

---

[290] R.P.George, "Lincoln on Judicial Despotism", *First Things*, February 2003, 36 at
p. 39–40.
[291] H.F.Stone, "The Common Law in the United States" (1936) 50 *Harvard Law
Review* 4 at p. 20.
[292] *Southern Pacific Co v Jensen* 244 U.S. 205, *per* Holmes J., at 221 (1917).
[293] A.R.Blackshield, "Quantitative Analysis: The High Court of Australia 1964–
1969" (1972) 3 *Lawasia* 1; G.Schubert, *Quantitative Analysis of Judicial Behaviour*
(The Freer Press, New York, 1959); G.Schubert, *The Judicial Mind* (Northwestern University Press, Evanston, 1965); J.A.G.Griffith, *The Politics of the
Judiciary* (Fontana, London, 5th ed., 1997); R.Stevens, *The English Judges: Their
Role in the Changing Constitution* (Hart Publishing, Oxford, 2002); cf. Zander,
op. cit., 223 above, p. 95 referring to D.Robertson, *Judicial Discretion in the House
of Lords* (Clarendon Press, Oxford, 1998).

high levels of consistency in judicial responses to particular categories of case. In turn, this suggests that, whatever judges say, deep-seated philosophical, social, psychological and even political considerations can affect judicial approaches to the resolution of legal problems, particularly in the higher appellate courts.

Of course, by referring to "political", I use that word as Justice Dixon did. Most issues of public law are "political" in one sense. I do not mean partisan or party political. From those activities of politics, judges of our tradition must be divorced. But in the higher courts especially, judges are inescapably part of the judicial branch of government. And that means they are part of politics viewed in the broad sense of that notion.

Perhaps recognising these realities, there are still some judges who think that the less said about policy considerations the safer they, and the judicial institution, will be. Whilst I acknowledge the sincerity of this opinion, it seems unlikely that "judicial illusionism"[294] can now be restored, assuming that to be a desirable goal, which I would contest. However imperfect may be the attempts in the last half century to confront the contextual and other considerations that influence judicial decisions, hiding them even from oneself is unlikely, in the future, to convince anyone that such influences do not exist.[295]

A controlling consideration that limits the occasions and extent of judicial lawmaking is the dependence of judges on the presentation of a case. Typically, it is the parties who tender an issue and invite a novel approach or a new rule.[296] A judge must also give reasons that are publicly available. In a collegiate court such reasons are subject to dissenting opinions. They are exposed to public, political, media and peer group criticism if the reasons are viewed as unconvincing.[297] The very fact that some judges now feel able to reveal and justify policy considerations that sustain the choices they make, can sometimes act as a brake on illegitimate or excessive lawmaking which the presentation of the subject, as nothing but an extension of "doctrine" or the strictly logical requirement of earlier judicial words, may serve to disguise.[298]

At whatever level they may be in the hierarchy, judges of the common law tradition, are aware of the superior right of the

---

[294] P.Atiyah, "Judges and Policy" (1980) 15 *Israel Law Review* 346; in R.Cooke, "Fairness" (1989) 19 *University of Victoria Wellington Law Review* 421.

[295] Atiyah, *op. cit.*, n. 80, p. 155.

[296] Sackville, *op. cit.*, n. 41 above, p. 67.

[297] Hayne, *op. cit.*, n. 281 above, p. 16; Handler, *op. cit.*, n. 112 above, at p. 308.

[298] V.Waye, "Justiciability" in *Australian Studies in Law—Administrative Law* (M.Harris and V.Waye eds., Federation Press, Sydney, 1991), at p. 47.

legislature and its special legitimacy to make laws within its constitutional competence, particularly involving major changes to the law. Large questions of policy; subjects of high political controversy; issues raising complex points of detail; and the prospect of exceptions necessitating study and empirical research beyond the evidence given in the particular case will not normally seem appropriate for legal change through the techniques of common law elaboration.[299]

Where a principle of the common law is one of longstanding, particularly where it constitutes a settled or fundamental rule[300] or a rule upon which many people might be expected to have ordered their affairs or assessed their rights, judges will generally leave it alone. In such cases, judges of the common law will normally prefer restraint.[301] Even where a persuasive case is made out to suggest that the established rule is unjust or inadequate, judges will commonly leave it to the legislature to provide any repair. Sometimes, the judges may recommend the need for legislative reform. Occasionally, they may indicate a willingness to contemplate judicial re-expression of a rule of the common law in the future, if the legislature fails to act.[302]

However, the foregoing description of what is usually the case necessarily allows for exceptions. To some observers of the judiciary, this is a good thing and an assurance of adaptability of the law in the pursuit of justice, something more than rules for their own sake. Lord Alexander of Weedon, for instance, in defending the judiciary against ministerial attack, recently said:

> "We should be saying thank goodness for our judges. Let's be grateful for them. To undermine the judiciary when the government has a huge majority and when there is no effective opposition and we have an elected dictatorship, is to create a real danger of a vacuum in the constitutional brakes on executive power".[303]

---

[299] *Ross v McCarthy* [1970] N.Z.L.R. 449; *Trigwell, op. cit.,* n. 30 above; Smillie, *op. cit.,* n. 177, at p. 273.

[300] Winfield, *op. cit.,* n. 83 above, p. 100 ("The lines of the trunk are settled whatever may be the direction of its new branches"). In *Mabo, op. cit.,* n. 34 above, Brennan J. (at 29–30) referred to the unchangeable core as the "skeleton" of the common law.

[301] *Gutnick, op. cit.,* n. 238 above, at 614–615, 629–635, *per* Kirby J. In the United States, the elaborated concept of judicial restraint is usually traced to J.B.Thayer, "The Origin and Scope of the American Doctrine of Constitutional Law" (1893) 7 *Harvard Law Review* 129. The concept was developed by Bickel, *op. cit.,* n. 266 above.

[302] This was effectively what happened in Australia in respect of judicial warnings about uncorroborated confessions to police. Following a series of decisions, the High Court ultimately laid down the rule of practice expressed in *McKinney v The Queen* (1991) 171 C.L.R. 468.

[303] Gibb, *op. cit.,* n. 269 above.

For every adherent to this opinion, in Britain, Australia and elsewhere, there are others who call for still more stringent controls on judicial creativity. One Australian writer even mused about the possibility of making judicial activism a disciplinary offence; drawing back only because of his concern that it might have a chilling effect on judicial independence.[304] Perhaps he was joking. But the idea of disciplining judges on such grounds is not as unusual as it might seem. In the United States, several attempts were made to impeach Chief Justice Warren and Justice Douglas of the Supreme Court. Fortunately, none succeeded.

Some commentators have argued the need for Commonwealth countries to learn from the United States and to subject senior judicial appointees to public scrutiny in order to elicit any previously undisclosed or unidentified policy values that may, upon appointment, emerge to influence their judicial performance.[305] In most common law countries, the spectacle of the confirmation hearings of Judges Bork and Thomas in the United States has put a dampener on the enthusiasm for this innovation. The serious backlog in judicial nominations in the United States under Presidents Clinton and G. W. Bush, based on politically partisan and specific issue lines, has tended to reinforce this sense of caution about legislative involvement in the process of judicial appointments.

On the other hand, change is in the air. In South Africa, candidates for senior judicial office are interviewed publicly. The mechanism seems to have worked. In Australia and other countries, advertisements have appeared in relation to very senior judicial appointments.[306] The same has happened in Britain. The proposal for a Supreme Court of the United Kingdom includes discussion of the process for identifying future candidates for appointment.[307] In respect of recent appointments to the High Court of Australia, the Federal Attorney-General interviewed privately many judges and potential candidates.[308] His conduct gave rise to criticism on the ground of secret political "vetting". In view of the earlier

---

[304] Campbell, *op. cit.*, n. 5 above, p. 314.

[305] *ibid.*, at p. 326.

[306] The office of Chief Justice of Victoria was recently advertised and the practice of advertisement appears to be spreading in Australia. Likewise in England: Zander, *op. cit.*, n. 223 above, pp. 98–100.

[307] United Kingdom Department for Constitutional Affairs, *op. cit.*, n. 38 above, at p. 33. K.Malleson, "Assessing the Performance of the Judicial Services Commission" (1999) 116 *South African Law Journal* 36.

[308] Seemingly pursuant to the High Court of Australia Act 1979 (Cth), s. 6.

commitment by the deputy leader of the Government that only "Capital C Conservative[s]" would be appointed to the High Court, it is unsurprising that the process of private interviews should have proved controversial.[309] Yet even those sceptical about the United States system perceive a shift in Commonwealth countries to a more open procedure. In part, this is nothing more than a result of the more open acknowledgment of the inescapable impact of policy on much judicial decision-making.[310]

HUMAN RIGHTS ON A GLOBAL SCALE

Platitudes about the need for judicial restraint or deference to the legislature do not advance very far the dialogue about the true character of our constitutional system, including the part that judges play in it.[311] In a modern democracy, this means conceiving the role and limits of law, viewing its operation within society as it exists and as it could be, and considering its institutions against the yardstick of universal human rights.

The principles of human rights typically pull us in different directions. On the one hand, they may suggest that a rule of the common law, an interpretation of statute or even of the constitution, breaches a fundamental principle of human rights. On the other hand, one settled human rights principle is addressed to the judiciary itself. It requires not only that judges should be *competent* and *independent* but also that they should be *impartial* in the discharge of their duties.[312] The last-mentioned principle helps to remind judges that they have no rights, as an elected legislator may, to pursue an agenda that they conceive to be in the interests of society. They are adjudicators. They must approach the resolution of the parties' dispute without partiality toward either side. Nor must they be obedient to external interest.[313]

---

[309] C.Merritt, "Court row as Williams vets judges", *Australian Financial Review*, December 11, 2002, p. 1; D.Solomon, "A Courtly Brawl", *Courier Mail*, February 27, 2003, p. 15.

[310] R.Davis and G.Williams, "Reform of the Judicial Appointments Process; Gender and the Bench of the High Court of Australia" (2003) 27:3 *Melbourne University Law Review* 819.

[311] Justice, *op. cit.*, n. 41 above, p. 305; cf. Doyle, *op. cit.*, n. 7 above, at p. 93.

[312] *International Covenant on Civil and Political Rights*, art. 14.1.

[313] *e.g. Karttunen v Finland* [1992] I.I.H.R.L. 53 (October 23, 1992) (U.N.H.R.C); *Fey v Austria* [1993] I.I.H.R.L. 7 (February 24, 1993) (Eur. Ct. H.R.); *Gregory v United Kingdom*, [1996] I.I.H.R.L. 19 (February 25, 1996) (Eur. Ct. H.R.) and other cases in *International Human Rights Law and Practice* (F.F.Martin *et al* ed., Kluwer Law International, 1997), p. 527.

Inescapably, every judge will have attitudes, opinions, even perhaps a coherent philosophy. Psychiatrists may tell us that these considerations inevitably influence the perception of problems and thus affect their solutions. But a judge is a special decision-maker. So far as humanly possible, he or she must keep an open mind, consciously avoiding partiality, pre-judgment or the appearance of these things.[314]

As the Supreme Court of Canada has pointed out[315] impartiality does not mean total *neutrality* about all subjects that come before the courts. It is not necessary for a judge to be neutral to violence and other breaches of fundamental rights whilst being impartial in the resolution of a contest concerning a party's alleged breach of such norms. In most countries today, a list of fundamental human rights is contained in the written constitution or, as in Canada, in an associated *Charter*. In other countries, such as the United Kingdom and New Zealand,[316] the fundamental rights are collected in a statute which is given a special status.

Australia has so far adopted neither of these approaches. But this does not mean that Australian judges are cut off entirely from the influence on judicial decision-making in contemporary human rights law. In construing legislation designed to protect people from human rights abuses, close attention is often given by the High Court and other courts in Australia to principles that are contained in international and comparative law.[317] The facility of complaint to the United Nations Human Rights Committee, where Australian law is shown to be in breach of the *International Covenant on Civil and Political Rights*, has stimulated not only legislative change (to remove the non-compliance).[318] It has sometimes influenced judicial exposition of the common law.[319] It may also affect the interpretation of local legislation.[320]

---

[314] D.A.Ipp, "Judicial impartiality and judicial neutrality: Is there a difference?" (2000) 19 *Australian Bar Review* 212.

[315] *R. v RDS* [1997] 3 S.C.R. 484; (1997) 151 D.L.R. 4th 193.

[316] Human Rights Act 1998 (UK); New Zealand Bill of Rights Act 1990 (NZ).

[317] *Jumbunna Coal Mine v Victorian Coalminers' Association* (1908) 6 C.L.R. 309, *per* O'Connor J., at 363; A.F.Mason, "The Internationalisation of Domestic Law" Law and Policy Paper No. 4 (Centre for International and Public Law, Australian National University, Canberra, 1996).

[318] I.Shearer, "United Nations Human Rights Committee: The *Toonen Case*" (1995) 69 *Australian Law Journal* 600.

[319] Bennion, *op. cit.*, n. 52 above, pp. 698 *et seq.* See *Mabo, op. cit.*, n. 34 above, *per* Brennan J., at 42; *Dietrich, op. cit.*, n. 194 above, *per* Mason C.J. and McHugh J., at 300, referring to the European Convention on Human Rights, art. 6 and the I.C.C.P.R., art. 14.

[320] Young, *op. cit.*, n. 258 above; cf. R.Clayton, "The Limits of What's 'Possible': "Statutory Construction under the *Human Rights Act*" [2002] 5 *European Human Rights Law Review* 559 at p. 564.

The use by judges of international human rights law has obvious limits. Under our constitutional arrangements, in the absence of legislation permitting that course, it is not for a judge to import a treaty, or treaty obligations, into municipal law "by the back door".[321] If the applicable municipal law is clear, unincorporated provisions of international instruments will not, of themselves, invalidate that law. This is certainly so if the law exists in statutory form.[322] However, these rules leave a great deal of scope for a judge of the common law to have regard to the developments of human rights jurisprudence in shaping the present content, and future directions, of a nation's common law.[323]

Even before the Human Rights Act in the United Kingdom, judges were using human rights law in expounding the content of the common law.[324] Despite the critics of this process,[325] it is natural and inevitable that contemporary judges should have regard to this large body of international legal principle.[326] We will see more of it. The new body of international law provides a source for consistent judicial decision-making where there is a gap to be filled in the common law or an ambiguity of the written law to be resolved. Better by far to utilise this developed body of principle, elaborated by highly trained lawyers in reasoned decisions, than to be captives forever of dimly remembered lessons in morality learned by the judge at a parent's knee forty years before.

The economic and social forces of globalisation are relevant to these developments. The ethical and policy debates that occur in

---

[321] *Teoh, op. cit.*, n. 34 above, *per* Mason C.J. and Deane J., at 291; Parkinson, *op. cit.*, n. 13 above, p. 185.

[322] Young, *op. cit.*, n. 258 above, *per* Kirby P, at 280–281. *Ex parte Brind* [1991] 1 A.C. 696, *per* Lord Donaldson, at 717; cf. Zander, *op. cit.*, n. 223 above, at 92.

[323] M.Allars, "International Law and Administrative Discretion" in *International Law and Australian Federalism* (B.Opeskin and D.Rothwell, Melbourne University Press, Melbourne, 1997), p. 232 at pp. 258 *et seq.*; M.D.Kirby, "The Australian Use of International Human Rights Norms: From Bangalore to Balliol—A View from the Antipodes" (1993) 16 *University of New South Wales Law Journal* 363; A.M.Gleeson, "Global Influences on the Australian Judiciary" (2002) 22 *Australian Bar Review* 184.

[324] B.Opeskin, "Constitutional Modelling: The Domestic Effect of International Law on Commonwealth Countries" (2001) 27 *Commonwealth Law Bulletin* 1242 referring to cases such as *Derbyshire County Council v Times Newspapers* [1992] Q.B. 770. See also Zander, *op. cit.*, n. 223 above, p. 91–93.

[325] Craven, *op. cit.* n. 161 above, p. 239; Heydon, *op. cit.*, n. 37 above, at p. 131; J. Kinslor, "'Killing Off' International Human Rights Law: An Exploration of the Australian Government's Relationship with United Nations Human Rights Committees" (2002) 8 *Australian Journal of Human Rights* 79.

[326] J.Perry, "Have the Judges Gone Too Far?: Courts versus the People" (2003) 15:4 *Judicial Officers' Bulletin* (NSW) 25.

national, regional and international courts and tribunals now represent an important element of today's legal and ethical environment. The common law, expressed by the judges, has always been sensitive to its intellectual and ethical context. An indication of the strong advance of this development can be seen in two recent decisions of the United States Supreme Court. In *Atkins v Virginia*,[327] universal human rights law was invoked by the majority of the Court in its reasons that struck down a State law providing for capital punishment in the case of a mentally handicapped prisoner. In *Lawrence v Texas*, decisions of the European Court of Human Rights were relied upon by the majority in support of the decision invalidating a state law criminalising adult private homosexual conduct.[328] In each case, Justice Scalia, in the minority, condemned the invocation of legal developments happening outside the American jurisdiction.

For the majority in *Lawrence*, the international and regional human rights law constituted a statement of "values share[d] with a wider civilisation".[329] When United States law, notoriously isolationist and self-contained, begins to draw on legal advances of this kind, it suggests the high persuasiveness and utility of universal human rights law as a source of basic principle in common law reasoning. Such material does not bind or coerce the municipal judge. But it is part of the intellectual and legal context in which judicial decisions will increasingly be made.

As national and international determinations come to influence courts in many lands, global sources will supplement purely local ones in judicial reasoning, especially when the judge is faced by a novel problem.[330] As Lord Steyn has put it, the *Universal Declaration of Human Rights*, after 1948, represented a "distillation of ethical values".[331] The marvellous adaptability of the judicial method of the common law permits judges, with and without domestic legislation, to have regard to such

---

[327] 536 U.S. 304 *per* Stevens J., at 329 (fn. 21) (2002).

[328] *op. cit.*, n. 162 above, *per* Kennedy J., at 4578–4580. In *Bowers v Hardwick* 478 U.S. 186 (1986), an earlier case on adult homosexual rights, Powell J. said that only a "facetious" interpretation of the Constitution would produce the outcome now adopted. Reportedly, Powell J. later regretted his opinion in *Bowers*. For equivalent developments in the United Kingdom see *Mendoza v Ghaidan* [2002] 4 All E.R. 1162.

[329] *op. cit.*, n. 162 above, at 4579. These developments have predictably drawn sharp criticism in a new book by Robert Bork, *Coercing Virtue: the Worldwide Rule of Judges* (AEIP, LaVergne, 2003).

[330] C.Taylor, *Sources of the Self: The Making of the Modern Identity* (Harvard University Press, 1989), p. 313.

[331] Lord Steyn, *op. cit.*, n. 166 above, p. 19.

developments in finding and expressing local principles of law. In the age of atomic energy, cyberspace and the human genome, the common law must resist the pettifogging demand of traditional formalists to return our legal system to the self-satisfied legal nationalism of the past. In today's world, that approach represents an appeal for return to an age that is no more.[332]

The incorporation of universal human rights principles into common law reasoning constitutes a significant change for the legal systems of the Commonwealth of Nations.[333] However, the common law, like the English language, has a seemingly inexhaustible capacity of absorption. Judges, who live in an age when the idea of universal human rights has come to be accepted, if not always practised, will not be impervious to the resulting scholarship and jurisprudence. They will mould, adapt and use it in proper ways in performing their judicial functions, just as they have done with other sources in the past.[334]

It is true that universal human rights law may sometimes be counter-majoritarian. Sadly, prejudice and discrimination are endemic to human society. But contemporary democratic theory recognises the importance of protecting the basic rights of minorities, not just upholding the will of the majority.[335] Critics with unsophisticated conceptions of modern democracy[336] need to be encouraged to study how representative democracy actually works. Within such a democracy, at least in common law countries, there is a proper role for judicial creativity. That judiciary is as much a part of the organs of a democratic government as are the other branches. It is not elected. But it is publicly accountable in other ways.

CONSTITUTIONAL INTERPRETATION

Learning to live with the reality of policy choices is also an feature of the judicial interpretation of written constitutional

---

[332] cf. Gleeson, *op. cit.*, n. 323 above, at p. 187. There remain constraints: J.Young, "The Constitutional Limits of Judicial Activism: Judicial Conduct of International Relations and Child Abduction" (2003) 66 *Modern Law Review* 823 at p. 836.

[333] Zander, *op. cit.*, n. 223 above, p. 78; Palley, *op. cit.*, n. 249 above, p. 112.

[334] Palley, *op. cit.*, n. 249 above, pp. 156–157 gives a fine illustration from the position before the Human Rights Act 1998 (UK) commenced operation in Northern Ireland. Lord Lowry C.J. invoked human rights norms in an important decision in the trial of I.R.A. suspects.

[335] Contrast *Dennis*, *op. cit.*, n. 180 above, with *Australian Communist Party Case*, *op. cit.*, n 152 above.

[336] *e.g.* Campbell, *op. cit.*, n. 5 above, at 325; Gava, *op. cit.*, n. 219 above, 748.

texts. A dwindling band of legal fundamentalists believes in
constitutional interpretation according to the original intent of
the writers of the document.[337] There are other variations on
their theme.[338] But given the increasing unwillingness of courts
to interpret social legislation in terms of the "intent" of those
who enacted the statute years or decades earlier,[339] the endeavour to inflict such formalism on the interpretation of a national
constitution is increasingly regarded by most judges as unten-
able. Of its nature, a constitutional text must adapt and apply to
completely new and unforeseen national and international circumstances as the constitution, if successful, outlives those who
wrote it.

No-one in Australia really believes that it is possible to
interpret the federal Constitution by reference only to its words
and without regard to the implications and structure of the
document as an instrument of government of a particular kind.
When Justice Dixon led the majority of the High Court of
Australia to invalidate the federal legislation of 1951 that sought
to dissolve the Australian Communist Party and to impose civil
burdens on its members, he did so on the footing, not of express
words in the constitutional text but on the basis of a broad
political and philosophical *concept* of the rule of law. This rule of
law was, he said, an "assumption" of the Constitution. This put
unexpressed controls upon the ambit of the federal lawmaking
power.[340]

Because this was an inescapable conclusion from the reasoning and outcome of that important case,[341] defenders of Dixon's
formalistic proposition that positive law dictates the decision in
all cases of constitutional conflict rely upon a verbal justification
for the great judge's creativity, as there in defence of individual
freedom. Their explanation is worthy of medieval theologians.
They say that the solution of a particular case is "generated
from within existing doctrine". Yet it necessarily remains for
judges to do the generation of such "doctrine". Commonly, they

---

[337] Craven, *op. cit.*, n. 161 above, pp. 217–219.
[338] D.Dawson, "Intention and the Constitution—Whose Intent?" (1990) 6
Australian Bar Review 93; M.Bagaric, "Originalism: Why Some Things Should
Never Change—Or At Least Not Too Quickly" (2000) 19 *University of Tasmania
Law Review* 173; D.Meagher, "Guided by Voices? Constitutional Interpretation
on the Gleeson Court" (2002) 7 *Deakin Law Review* 261.
[339] *e.g. Fitzpatrick v Sterling Homes Ltd* [2001] 1 A.C. 27, *per* Lord Nicholls, at 45;
Mendoza, op. cit., n. 327 above; cf. I.Loveland, "Making it up as They Go
Along? The Court of Appeal on Same-Sex Spouses and Succession Rights to
Tenancies" [2003] *Public Law* 222.
[340] Zines, *op. cit.*, n. 151 above, p. 13.
[341] *Australian Communist Party, op. cit.* n. 152 above.

must fulfil that task using a multitude of sources. Many of those sources are difficult to reconcile. Where, in a dispute, the words of the constitutional text are ambiguous, the only way of deriving the necessary "doctrine" is by the judges choosing between competing interpretations. Not uncommonly, those interpretations rest upon constitutional values that are unexpressed. Often such values will be conflicting. Commonly they will be highly controversial.[342]

Given the need to have an umpire in disputes about the meaning of a written constitution, where the interests of powerful forces collide, and given the assignment of that role in most modern democracies to courts, there is no escaping the deeply political character of the function thereby handed to the judges. Even Justice Frankfurter, a supposed paragon of judicial restraint, acknowledged:[343] "The process of constitutional interpretation compels the translation of policy into judgment". An acceptance that that is so in countries that live under a written constitution, may suggest implications for the selection and tenure of the judges who enjoy such a large power. But, so far as the method of their decision-making is concerned, it also suggests the need for self-awareness and transparency in the identification of the assumptions that lead them to particular decisions. Such decisions need to be anchored in the constitutional text. However, pretending that the solution can be found in the words of that text alone, or in a supposed "doctrine", is unlikely to convince the increasingly better informed and critical readers of modern judicial opinions.[344]

BE NOT AFRAID

There are many lessons to be learned from the legal Reformation and Counter-Reformation over the judicial method. They

---

[342] *Western Australia v The Commonwealth* (1976) 134 C.L.R. 201; *Queensland v The Commonwealth* (1977) 139 C.L.R. 585. In these cases concerning the statutory creation of Territorial senators, the Court had to choose between upholding the federal principle in the *Australian Constitution* favouring the States and the principle of representative democracy favouring the validity of the senators. See Zines, *op. cit.*, n. 151 above, at p. 14. The majority favoured the latter.

[343] Cited G.Winterton "*Should the High Court consider Policy?*" (1998) *Australian Journal of Public Administration* 73 at p. 74. But see G.E.White, "Felix Frankfurter's 'Soliloquy' in *Ex parte Quirin*" (2003) 2d: 5 *The Green Bag* 433 at p. 33, which points out what an "activist" Frankfurter J. really was.

[344] R.Hirschl, "Resituating the Globalisation of Politics: *Bush v Gore* as a Global Trend" (2002) 15 *Canadian Journal of Law and Jurisprudence* 191 at 215.

include the need for judges of the common law to proceed in a principled manner when asked to re-express the law in a way that changes past formulations.[345]

In some circumstances there are special reasons for action or for restraint, some of which I have mentioned.[346] Numerous attempts have been made to catalogue them. In an earlier century, efforts were made to expound exhaustively the parts of the law in which "public policy" considerations could play a role.[347] Today the search goes on for the factors that encourage, or restrain, judicial re-expression of the law in ways that affect the rights of the parties and others in a like position. The quest for an exhaustive checklist is an illusion. The judge who cries in dissent for restraint in one case may be moved in another to lead the court's efforts to re-express the law. The judge's analysis may bring him or her to discard past statements of legal authority as "ill adapted to modern circumstances . . . [or] rest[ing] on dubious foundations".[348] Yet in the next case, the same judge may reject the appeal to a like creativity and insist on strict adherence to past "doctrine" and settled legal authority.

We should not be over-concerned about such divergences. Obviously, a general consistency of approach is desirable. However, a human institution like the judiciary, of changing membership and changing minds, operates within and serves a changing society. Over time, the judiciary is bound to reflect different values. The same judges may do so at different stages of their careers. In the common law system, this feature is institutionally entrenched by the right to dissent and by the practice of multiple opinions.[349] As the impact the philosophy of judges has upon their decisions becomes clearer to governments, it is natural and inevitable that governments should attempt to appoint, as judges, people whom they hope will reflect generally the values they hold dear. But if, once appointed, the judge is competent, independent and impartial, he or she will often disappoint those who seek to categorise an appointee by simple stereotypes.

---

[345] Lord Bingham, *op. cit.*, n. 115 above, p. 10.
[346] cf M.D.Kirby, *Through the World's Eye* (Federation, Sydney, 2000), p. 93. Lord Devlin instanced judicial intrusions into "highly controversial subjects": Devlin, *op. cit.*, n. 133 above, pp. 9–10.
[347] Handler, *op. cit.*, n. 112 above, pp. 303–305.
[348] *Wik, op. cit.*, n. 201 above, *per* Gummow J. at 179–180. See Kirby, *op. cit.*, n. 106 above, pp. 10–14.
[349] R. Smyth, "Historical Consensual Norms in the High Court" (2001) 37 *Australian Journal of Political Science* 215 at pp. 259, 264.

Judges must necessarily decide cases that involve unique facts. They must respond, as their vocation obliges, to the parties' arguments. It is the obligation to make a decision in a particular case, affecting real parties, that concentrates the judicial mind on the duty to find, as accurately and efficiently as possible, the applicable rule of legal authority.[350] If that rule is clear and binding, the judge normally applies it. And that is that. The cases where the propounded rule is unclear, not binding or such as to suggest the need for a court with the power to do so to re-express it, is exceptional. The higher the judge is placed in the judicial hierarchy, the more likely is it that such exceptional cases will arise for decision.

When they do, the common law judge is not bereft of a principled solution to the problem before the court. In our "eclectic" methodology of decision-making,[351] the judge can look to several sources for guidance. In an age of legislative dominance, the judge can seek inspiration from the text of the constitution,[352] if there is one, or from relevant statutes that appear to support a general principle.[353] Or the judge may have regard to a wide range of resources of which judicial notice may be taken.[354] In some places the judge may have the benefit of a Brandeis brief (or its local equivalent) by which he or she may gain a better understanding of the policy behind the law.[355] Or the judge may look (as increasingly we all do) to decisions on analogous problems in countries with similar legal systems[356] or even those with legal systems different from our own.

In matters involving judge-made law, concerned with issues of court practice and procedure, with which the judge may be familiar, it will frequently be possible for the judge to draw on personal experience.[357] Beyond such cases, the judge will generally be left to rely upon the arguments of the parties and the

---

[350] Mason, *op. cit.*, n. 44 above, p. 15; cf. Atiyah, *op. cit.*, n. 80 above, p. 173.

[351] Barak, *op. cit.*, n. 280 above, p. 94.

[352] *Roberts, op. cit.*, n 203 above, *per* Kirby J., at 55.

[353] Winfield, *op. cit.*, n. 83 above, p. 97.

[354] *Australian Broadcasting Corporation v Lenah Game Meats Pty Ltd* (2001) 208 C.L.R. 199, *per* Callinan J., at 298.

[355] M.Lavarch, "How the High Court Considers Policy" (1998) *Australian Journal of Public Administration* 86 at p. 88; Lord Irvine, "The Impact of the *Human Rights Act*" [2003] *Public Law* 308 at 326 referring to *Brown v Stott* [2001] 2 W.L.R. 817.

[356] *e.g. New South Wales v Lepore* (2003) 77 A.L.J.R. 558; 195 A.L.R. 412 concerning liability of schools for sexual misconduct of teachers. The Court drew upon *Bazley v Curry* [1999] 2 S.C.R. 534 (Canada) and *Lister v Hesley Hall Ltd* [2002] 1 A.C. 215 (United Kingdom).

[357] cf. *Gulf Oil Corporation v Gilbert* 330 U.S. 501 (1946).

rhetorical devices they deploy,[358] including any reference their advocates make to legal or social philosophers.[359] One of the most important lessons I have learned from commentaries on these lectures as they were given, was the significance of change in the judicial method for legal education and legal practice. Law faculties and professional training courses need to include instruction in how professional lawyers, by evidence and argument, can help judges to resolve policy choices in an informed and principled way. In the future, the citation of old cases without attention to consideration of legal principle and legal policy will increasingly be seen as inadequate. This is a great challenge to law teachers and practitioners. It demands attention, at least in the higher appellate courts, to argumentation of a new and somewhat different character.

In the end comes the application of an individual or collegiate decision based upon a mass of data perceived through the eyes of the decision-maker's understandings of the facts and the law viewed, in turn, through a prism of the judge's experiences, attitudes and values. In the case of most decision-makers there is an additional imperative. It is one that is reinforced by judicial duty, wherever possible, to find outcomes that seem just and reasonable, as well as lawful.

There are mean-spirited and callous members of the judiciary, as of any profession.[360] Some rare birds I have known actually delight in arriving at a result that is obviously unfair: proclaiming it with crocodile tears and pious solecisms about judicial restraint, deference and obedience to the law.

Every judge of any experience has had to give effect to unpalatable laws. It should not be a matter of satisfaction or indifference. It is a matter of duty. In some circumstances there may be something that the judge can do about it. In most countries today the new law of human rights may enlarge the judge's armoury for such hard cases. Those of a formalistic bent may not bother about apparent injustice. Outmoded statements of the law usually favour the powerful over the weak and vulnerable. Those who have hardened their hearts will not care a jot. But in cases of obvious injustice, a judge may feel impelled, and authorised, to avoid a clearly unjust outcome. These are the cases that Justice Oliver Wendell Holmes Jr., described as his "can't helps".[361] Yet, in every judge's life,

---

[358] M.K.Komesar, *Imperfect Alternatives* (University of Chicago Press, Chicago, 1994), p. 270.

[359] Atiyah, *op. cit.*, n. 80 above, p. 166.

[360] Justice, *op. cit.*, n. 41 above, p. 311.

[361] Cited A Lewis, Foreword to M Kozlowski, *The Myth of the Imperial Judiciary* (N.Y.U. Press, New York, 2003), p. xii.

fidelity to the fundamental requirements of the law will sometimes oblige an outcome that seems seriously wrong. Here too
the judge just "can't help" it.

Every country has important cases that present great choices
to the judges of that country's final court. Every lawyer can
identify such cases. One, in Australia, was the *Communist Party
Case*. Another was *Mabo* which affirmed native title. Another
was *The Queen v L*[362] in which the ancient immunity of husbands
from criminal liability for rape of their wives was found no
longer to be part of the common law of Australia. Faced with
such cases, judges cannot escape the obligation of choice and
decision. Reference to the "abiding values of contemporary
society", as an explanation for reformulation of previously
settled law, leaves judges who use such words open to the
criticism that they have mis-stated society's values. Or that their
intuition is imperfect. Or that their experience was too limited.
Or that their action was illegitimate.[363] Or that they are "judicial
activists".

Contemporary judges should not worry too much about such
criticisms. For centuries, the judges of the common law have
been reflecting, in a necessarily general way, the values of the
societies that they serve. As Patrick Atiyah explained,[364] when
the body of the law of contract emerged from the judges of
England in the eighteenth century those judges were greatly
influenced by the needs, and rapid development, of the English
economy at that time. Their decisions were significantly affected
by the theories of political economy of Adam Smith. In a similar
way, the judicial abolition of spousal immunity for rape, without
waiting for legislative change, was informed by strong contemporary advances in the recognition of the rights of women; by
close scrutiny of some of the old assumptions of the criminal
law that underpinned the former immunity; by changes in the
nature and incidents of marriage; and by global developments
resulting in the ratification of human rights treaties designed to
protect women.[365]

In such a changed world, it was intolerable to expect contemporary judges to give effect to the old rule, made by predecessors centuries earlier. In re-expressing the law to bring spousal

[362] (1991) 174 C.L.R. 379; Mason, *op. cit.*, n. 44 above, p. 9; Callinan, *op. cit.*, n. 124
above, p. 99; cf. *Gillick v West Norfolk Area Health Authority* [1986] A.C. 112, *per*
Lord Scarman, at 182–183.

[363] Smillie, *op. cit.*, n. 177 above, p. 261.

[364] Atiyah, *op. cit.*, n. 80 above, p. 168.

[365] For a like decision in the House of Lords see *R. v R.* [1992] 1 A.C. 599; cf.
Convention for the Elimination of All Forms of Discrimination Against
Women. Australia is a party to the *Convention* but not to the Optional Protocol
permitting individual complaint: Kinslor, *op. cit.*, n. 325 above.

victims within the protection of the law against non-consensual sexual assaults, today's judges were as true to the society of their time as their predecessors had been to theirs in a different time. The law was re-stated for compelling reasons. The Court felt able to do so with precision in a small and defined field of the law's operation.[366] True, the judges thereby effectively removed a previous legal immunity. Without the authority of statute, they effectively imposed retrospective criminal liability on the husband and doubtless others. But in doing so, they gave voice to what would have been the overwhelming opinion of contemporary society. Moreover, they did so in a branch of the common law that was, relevantly, the responsibility of the judges. Who will say that the judges were wrong to redefine the common law in that way? Be sure that some would denounce such action as egregious "judicial activism". If so, it is an epithet that the judges will gladly bear.

AUTHORITY, PRINCIPLE AND POLICY

Faced with a novel problem of the common law or an ambiguity in written law, the judge of our tradition will therefore have regard to three great sources of guidance: legal authority, legal principle and legal policy.[367] Depending on the judge's court, the problem may be resolved wholly by the application of binding legal authority. Even in a final court, if the authority is of longstanding or unsuitable for judicial change, the judge will generally apply it to the case in hand. That is the common law system of precedent and *stare decisis*.

Yet in some cases there will be no authority exactly on the point. The analogies of the common law will be remote, uncertain or unhelpful. Any applicable written law will be ambiguous or not really suitable to the case. The constitution will be silent. Then a judge of the common law tradition, especially in an appellate court, may search for guidance from legal principle and legal policy.

---

[366] Parkinson, *op. cit.*, n. 13 above, p. 191 referring to *Trident General Insurance Co Ltd v McNiece Bros Pty Ltd* (1988) 165 C.L.R. 107, *per* Deane J., at 143.

[367] *Oceanic Sun Line Special Shipping Co Inc v Fay* (1988) 165 C.L.R. 197, *per* Deane J., at 252; *Northern Territory v Mengel* (1995) 185 C.L.R. 307, *per* Mason C.J., Dawson, Toohey, Gaudron and McHugh J.J., at 347; cf. *Fairchild v Glenhaven Funeral Services Ltd* [2003] 1 A.C. 32, *per* Lord Bingham, at 43 [8] ("principle"), 46 [114] ("authority"), 66 [33] ("policy"). See also, *per* Lord Hoffman, at 71 [48], 75 [64].

Legal principle is derived from a close analysis of the emerging common themes of multiple decisions in connected areas of the law.[368] Professor Ronald Dworkin, who has opposed judicial use of policy arguments, acknowledges the legitimacy of legal principle as a source of judicial development of the law.[369] Likewise, some judges, who feel uncomfortable about open reliance on considerations of policy, fully accept that, in unsettled portions of the law, legal principle, derived by analogy and reasoning from past authority, can offer guidance for judicial choice.[370] Legal principle is not the same as legal policy; but it is allied to it. When a legal rule has been adapted by a court of high authority from considerations of legal policy in a series of cases, it takes on the character of a legal principle. In this sense, legal principle is the distilled product of earlier considerations of authority and policy.

However, legal principle, being itself the captive of past experience, will not always be of great assistance. Where legal precept, precedent, authority and past principles offer an insufficient guide, policy becomes essential to the decision-making of judges.

In such circumstances, the quandary of judicial choice may be helped, and judicial reasons made more transparent, by the identification of the policy considerations that the judge takes into account.[371] For example, in deciding claims for damages for negligence, the basic formulation of the cause of action is, by now, well settled. But whether, in the particular case, a duty of care exists on the part of the defendant towards the plaintiff will often present a borderline problem. Commonly, that problem will not be solved by the verbal formulae found in old cases. A satisfactory solution will only emerge from the application of legal policy. There may be no exact precedent for the circumstances of the case. Whether the principles emerging from other cases are sufficient to affix a duty may be controversial. Verbal

---

[368] Atiyah, *op. cit.*, n. 80 above, p. 156.
[369] M. M. Feeley and E. L. Rubin, *Judicial Policy Making and the Modern State: How the Courts Reformed America's Prisons* (Cambridge University Press, Cambridge, 1998), p. 5; see also Bennion, *op. cit.*, n. 52 above, p. 165; Horrigan, *op. cit.*, n. 111 above, 44, where references are made to R.W.Dworkin, *Taking Rights Seriously* (Duckworth, London, 1977).
[370] Atiyah, *op. cit.*, n. 80 above, p. 156; cf. *McLoughlin v O'Brian* [1983] 1 A.C. 410; *Sidaway v Bethlem Royal Hospital* [1985] A.C. 871, *per* Lord Scarman, at 888; *Caltex Oil (Aust) Pty Ltd v The Dredge "Willemstad"* (1976) 136 C.L.R. 529, *per* Stephen J., at 567.
[371] Handler, *op. cit.*, n 112 above, p. 306.

formulae ("foreseeability", "proximity", "reliance", "vulnerability", or a combination of these "salient factors")[372] may leave the decision-maker unsatisfied or even confused.

In the end, many novel cases require judges with the responsibility for such decisions to evaluate the choices they make by reference to considerations of legal policy. Will the imposition of a duty of care in the circumstances impose indeterminate liability on an indeterminate class? Will it expose people unreasonably to liability to others? Will it result in intolerable economic burdens? Will it have adverse implications for the availability of liability insurance? Will it diminish legitimate freedom of action by people in the position of the defendant? Will it drive some useful participants out of a valuable market? Will refusing it leave a vulnerable party without redress reasonable to the circumstances?

In the past, such questions were commonly submerged in judicial reasoning expressed in formulaic terms. In most jurisdictions of the common law today, judges in the higher courts, evaluate new cases by reference not only to authority and emerging principle; but also to considerations of legal policy. Without candid attention to policy, the law will shuffle blindly from the decision in one case to another.[373] Judicial attention to considerations of policy is not new. What is new is the open acknowledgment of it; its exposure to scrutiny in the course of argument of the cases; and the transparent discussion of policy evaluation in the judicial reasoning that follows.

This development is the abiding legacy of the enlightenment that came with the legal Reformation in the latter part of the twentieth century. So far, it has survived the Counter-Reformation. Whilst judges must tread with care in the territory marked legal principle and legal policy, because each is indeterminate and often controversial, there will be no going back to the pretence that legal authority alone solves every legal problem. To this extent, the judicial method of the common law has been changed forever by the legal Reformation.

The most that the Counter-Reformation has achieved is to make contemporary judges more careful in selecting the circumstances in which re-expression of past legal authority is justified and in explaining that justification in the particular case. A

---

[372] *Bryan v Maloney* (1995) 182 C.L.R. 609, *per* Mason C.J., Deane and Gaudron J.J., at 618, 628; *Perre v Apand Pty Ltd* (1999) 198 C.L.R. 180, *per* Gummow J., at 255; cf. *per* Kirby J., at 275, with reference to *Caparo Plc v Dickman* [1990] 2 A.C. 605 at 642; *South Pacific Manufacturing Co Ltd v NZ Security Consultants* [1992] 2 N.Z.L.R. 282, *per* Cooke P., at 294–299.

[373] Atiyah, *op. cit.*, n 80 above, p. 157.

return to the world of "excessive legalism" is as impossible in 2003 as would be a return, in Russia, to the world of Brezhnev & Co. There can be no going back to the falsehoods, fictions and illusions of the age before judicial glasnost. There may be occasional nostalgia for the pseudo ideals of the old regime and for its discredited doctrines. But the world has moved on. Try as they might, the old brigade cannot restore their glory days.

CONCORD

In the *Book of Common Prayer*, the Collect for Peace begins, with the memorable words: "O God, who art the author of peace and lover of concord".[374] The Collect goes on to invoke God's help to overcome "the power of any adversaries". I have reason to know this prayer well. As a boy, I grew to adulthood in a leafy suburb of Sydney by name Concord. I was convinced that it was a place within the special affection of God. Concord is a beautiful word, even though we know from history that, like peace, it comes "dropping slow".[375] I hope that these lectures contribute to concord between intellectual adversaries.

But in the law, as in the world, lasting peace can only be built on foundations of truth and justice. Falsehood, deception and indifference to wrongs will not afford a stable foundation for any legal order—least of all, one as creative as the common law. When politicians, editorialists and jurists use "judicial activism" as a label and a curse, it is not enough to respond with disbelief at their naivety. It is necessary for those who are aware of legal history, and of our system of law, to lift their voices. To tell the truth about the choices that judges must make in discharging their functions. To explain that, whilst the judge is indeed no "ad hoc legislator",[376] the judicial task is inescapably a creative activity, and in that sense political.[377] Whilst mistakes can sometimes be made by going too far (or not far enough) those who urge the unmoving application of past understandings of the law are usually guilty of advocating a judicial activism of their own.

Legal conservatism can be a highly activist ideology.[378] The legal conservative is usually attempting to impose on a later age,

---

[374] From the Order for Morning Prayer in the *Book of Common Prayer*.
[375] W.B.Yeats, "The Lake Isle of Innisfree" in W.B.Yeats, *Collected Poems*, (Macmillan, London, 1982), p. 44.
[376] A.M.Gleeson, "Individualised Justice: The Holy Grail" (1995) 69 *Australian Law Journal* 421 p. 432.
[377] A.C.Hutchinson, "Heydon' Seek: Looking for Law in all the Wrong Places" (2003) 29:1 *Monash University Law Review* 85, p.96.
[378] D.Elliott, "Conservative Judicial Activism Comes to Canada: *Egale v Canada* (2003) 36 *University of British Columbia Law Review* 29, p. 42.

unchanged, the values, beliefs and opinions of judges of an earlier, different time with no questions asked. As Justice Douglas, of the United States Supreme Court, explained:

> "The search for a static security—in the law or elsewhere—is misguided . . . [because] the fact is that security can only be achieved through constant change, through the wise discarding of old ideas that have outlived their usefulness, and through the adapting of others to current facts".[379]

The experience of the legal Counter-Reformation teaches us the need for fuller justifications for judicial re-expression of the law. However, the attempt to restore reactionary theories about the judicial function and formalism as a cloak for a substantive agenda[380] must be defeated—just as all extremist positions must fail. The modern judge can take pride in the honest disclosure of the influences of legal policy and principle (in addition to legal authority) as part of the judicial method of those who led the legal Reformation. Their error was not the abandonment of the doctrine of "strict and complete legalism", which was well-meaning but dishonest. Their error lay in discarding the duplicity of earlier illusions,[381] without adequately preparing the public for the change in judicial technique.[382]

It was unsurprising that the common law, from its earliest days, assigned a lawmaking role to the judiciary. The constitutional culture in which its developed never embraced a rigid separation of powers. At the centenary conference of the High Court of Australia Professor Jane Stapleton offered this insight:

> "Walter Bagehot famously stated that 'the efficient secret of the English Constitution may be described as the close union . . . of the Executive and legislative powers' in the Cabinet. In my view, the common law world is now at a stage where we can admit that an equally vital secret of our constitutional arrangements is the close union of the judicial and legislative powers in the court of ultimate appeal and that our common law legal systems embrace a form of separation of powers doctrine that accommodates this".[383]

It was inevitable that the element of judicial lawmaking would diminish with the growth of democratic parliaments; yet

---

[379] W.O.Douglas, "Stare Decisis" (1949) 49 *Columbia Law Review* 735, p. 735.

[380] Hutchinson, *op. cit.*, n. 377 above, p. 93.

[381] Anatole France quoted in Frank, *op. cit.*, n. 106 above, p. 115 cited R.Finkelstein, "Decision-making in a Vacuum?" (2003) 29 *Monash University Law Review* 11, pp. 11–12.

[382] This was the view of Professor Brian Galligan, cited Finkelstein, *ibid.*, at p. 28.

[383] J.Stapleton, "The Golden Thread at the Heart of Tort Law" (2003) 24:2 *Australian Bar Review* 135 at 137–138.

re-emerge as those parliaments fell under the iron discipline of the Executive, once the legislators had elected the executive from their number. Even countries, like Australia, with a written Constitution that reflects in a sharper way the separation of the judicial power from the others, cannot eliminate the character of that power as one having distinct lawmaking responsibilities. Such is the legacy to the entire common law world of the judges of Britain.

TEACHING THE TRUTH

How then, in the face of renascent formalism and community ignorance about the judiciary and its ways, can the truth of our legal system be told, so that it will be understood by lawyer and citizen alike?

First, and most obviously, it is the responsibility of judges to drop the deception that law is mechanical. They must tell it as it is. They must do so, not just in private conversations with each other, but publicly, so that citizens and fellow lawyers can understand the true nature of the complex task in which judges are engaged, including its creative element. One way to do this, as Lord Reid taught[384] is by humour. The magic words "strict logic and high technique" are much less likely to be taken seriously, since Lord Reid exploded the formalist fairytale with his metaphor of Aladdin's cave.

There are other powerful exponents who laugh the formalists to scorn. Lord Atkin did so with the invocation of Humpty Dumpty in his famous dissent in *Liversidge v Anderson*.[385] More recently, Lord Justice Sedley in his Atkin Lecture portrayed with sardonic humour the successive responses of judges of differing traditions to the plight of Prometheus J., an activist judge, who fell into the river whilst deep in thought about new ways to make the government's life difficult. Poor old Prometheus simply wanted to be saved from his plight by a creative and compassionate lawyer.[386] Sadly, none appeared. The coroner absolved all of the drowned judge's colleagues for doing nothing, because all of them demonstrated very good reasons for their inactivity. Yet, as Lord Justice Sedley points out, in the words of Francis Cornford a century ago, "doing nothing has just as many consequences as doing something".[387]

---

[384] Lord Reid, *op. cit.*, n. 169 above.
[385] [1942] A.C. 206 at 245.
[386] S.Sedley, "On Never Doing Anything for the First Time" (Atkin Lecture, November 6, 2001), at p. 3.
[387] *ibid.*, at p. 5.

If humour does not do the trick, we must hope for enlightenment from plain speaking. From education of the public in the ways of their government. From explanation of the reasons for a measure of judicial activism and of the many benefits for justice that it has brought in our legal tradition over eight centuries. As Karl Llewellyn[388] put it so well:

> "It seems to me essential to the health of our law and legal work that student, bar and bench should know that the Grand Tradition of the Common Law is our rightful heritage and needs complete and conscious recapture".

The judicial method of common law countries does not always provide "right answers". But its traditions, practices and techniques set the limits and constraints within which judicial creativity and transparency must sit.

And Philip Areeda's instruction must be spread far and wide:

> "Not only do our courts occupy a peculiar role in administering the Constitution, but our legislatures are willing to legislate in extremely vague terms that delegate enormous policymaking discretion to the courts. In addition, of course, contemporary judges continue to expand the common law. The resulting quantity of judge-made law applying to such a wide range of affairs is staggering, as is the variety of knowledge necessary to deal with it."[389]

For those who believe that this is a futile exercise, in the face of hostile politicians, media, business and other sources of power, hope may be discovered in recent events.

One outcome of the centenary of the High Court of Australia, has been an increase in public discussion of what courts actually do. And understanding about the legitimacy, indeed necessity, of judicial action to secure just and rational outcomes to disputes. Acceptance of the formalists' truisms about "judicial activism" was strongly questioned in the popular media. In its place, a better realisation of the nature of the judicial function was evident. Thus, the Melbourne *Age*[390] intoned:

> "Over the years many politicians have chosen to criticise, and sometimes even severely attack, the judiciary for supposed interference with the intentions of parliamentary law-makers. Such

---

[388] Llewellyn (1951), *op. cit.* n. 7 above, p. 157.
[389] P.Areeda, "Always A Borrower: Law and Other Disciplines" (1988) *Duke Law Journal* 1029 at pp. 1031–1032.
[390] Editorial, "A pillar of Australia's democratic life" *The Age* (Melbourne), October 9, 2003, at p. 12.

accusations typically rest on the assumption that courts are not supposed to 'make' law: a rhetorically appealing line to some, but false nonetheless. The role of appellate courts, especially the High Court, is to resolve disputed questions, and it is inevitable that in the process of doing so they will make law".

The Adelaide *Advertiser*[391] commented, even more pointedly:

"Some politicians would like to believe they, and they alone, should make the laws in Australia and that it is not the responsibility or charter of the High Court to interpret the meaning and intent of those laws. But in resolving legal disputes the High Court followed the time-honoured traditions of British common law and in doing so at times recasts the original objective of Parliamentary law. Court rulings . . . have not always pleased governments but have become indelibly etched in law".

To similar effect were comments in many other media outlets, print and electronic. Perhaps we need more occasions to divert the media from their usual fare of sport, celebrities and scandal to encourage improved understanding of the judiciary and its work. Such knowledge is an antidote to the "rhetorically appealing line" pedalled by the formalists and strict legalists. It helps reinforce understanding of the law's essential social mission. With greater understanding, judges, lawyers and other citizens can concentrate, in a temperate dialogue, upon what should be the *real* debate over judicial activism: identification of the circumstances for action and of the occasions for restraint.

Where humour and rational explanations do not produce concord about judicial activism, a final means, a parable, may help.

THE PARABLE OF THE LAW'S GARDEN

The common law is not a formal garden. Like other gardens of the English tradition, it is not a place of manicured lawns, observing a strictly preordained theory with a coherent, formal design. Instead, it is a somewhat chaotic place. It is full of intricate delights and hidden joys as well as dark, secluded spots where swamps appear with clusters of thick weeds and mangrove trees to trap the unwary judicial traveller.

Only from above, from a great height, can the logic, pattern and essential order of this garden be perceived. The judicial

---

[391] Editorial, "A century of judicial independence" *The Advertiser* (Adelaide), October 10, 2003, at p. 16.

gardeners are busy. Basically they do not have much time, or the inclination, to change the place in substantial ways. Obviously, they must keep trimming and planting new beds for changing seasons. Those who use the garden usually rather like it the way it is, even when it becomes overgrown. It seems to suit the temperament of those who live and visit there. Every now and again the gardeners try to clean up a section of the garden. They pull out a few dead bushes. They replant the remainder in a more orderly fashion. When this happens, some of those who knew the garden as it was get extremely angry. A few, of curmudgeonly disposition, go round muttering that the former state of things should be restored. Some, who are upset, scream and shout at the gardeners. They denounce them as horticultural "activists". For a time these faithful retainers withdraw. Their forays into cleaning up tend to come in cycles.

But then things go on much as they have for centuries. The gardeners get a bug of inspiration. Armed with the many new tools that you can buy now, they go to work again. In recent times the gardeners have become much more aware of what they are doing. This may be because they have lately taken to reading books on the work of those with interesting gardens far away. Yet overall, things have not changed all that much. It is how this garden has been maintained for centuries. It is how it will probably be for centuries to come. The remarkable thing is that the garden, for all its many faults, is much admired. Those who live elsewhere, come and look over the wall. Sometimes they shake their heads at the apparent chaos and lack of logic and order; but in their hearts they know that the garden has been looking better in recent times. Indeed, there is probably no better garden in the world.

Bibliography

Allars, M., "International Law and Administrative Discretion" in *International Law and Australian Federalism* (B. Opeskin and D. Rothwell, Melbourne University Press, Melbourne, 1997)

Areeda, P., "Always A Borrower: Law and Other Disciplines" (1988) *Duke Law Journal* 1029

Ashworth, A., *Human Rights, Serious Crime and Criminal Procedure* (54th Hamlyn lectures, 2001) (Sweet & Maxwell, London, 2002)

Atiyah, P., "Judges and Policy" (1980) 15 *Israel Law Review* 346

Atiyah, P., *Pragmatism and Theory in English Law* (39th Hamlyn Lectures, 1987) (Stevens, London, 1977)

Ayres, P., *Owen Dixon: A Biography* (Miegunyah Press, Carlton, 2003)

Bacon, F., "Of Judicature" in *Essays Civil and Moral*

Bagaric, M., "Originalism: Why Some Things Should Never Change—Or At Least Not Too Quickly" (2000) 19 *University of Tasmania Law Review* 173

Barak, A., "A Judge on Judging: The Role of a Supreme Court in a Democracy" (2002) 116 *Harvard Law Review* 16

Baxi, U., "Taking Suffering Seriously: Social Action Litigation in the Supreme Court of India" (1980) 9 *Delhi Law Review* 91

Bellacosa, J.W., "Remarks—Judging Cases v Courting Public Opinion" (1997) 65 *Fordham Law Review* 2381

Bennion, F., *Statutory Interpretation* (4th ed., Butterworths, London, 2002)

Bickel, A., *The Least Dangerous Branch: The Supreme Court at the Bar of Politics* (2nd ed., Yale University Press, New Haven, 1986)

Bingham, T., "The Judge as Lawmaker: An English Perspective" in *The Struggle for Simplicity in the Law—Essays for Lord Cooke of Thorndon* (P. Rishworth ed., Butterworths, Wellington, 1997)

Binnie, I., "The Future of Equality", Paper for a Conference on Liberty, Equality, Community: Constitutional Rights in Conflict? (Auckland, 1999)

Blackshield, A.R., "Quantitative Analysis: The High Court of Australia 1964–1969" (1972) 3 *Lawasia* 1

Blackstone, W., *Commentaries on the Laws of England* (15th ed, T. Cadell and W. Davies, London, 1809) Vol 1

Bork, R., *Coercing Virtue: the Worldwide Rule of Judges* (AEIP, LaVergne, 2003)

Bright, S.B., "Political Attacks on the Judiciary" (1997) 80 *Judicature* 165

Bright, S.B., "Political Attacks on the Judiciary: Can Justice be Done Amidst Efforts to Intimidate or Remove Judges from Office for Unpopular Decisions?" (1997) 72 *New York University Law Review* 308

Brooks, R.L., "The Use of Policy in Judicial Reasoning: A Reconceptualization Before and After *Bush v Gore*" (2002) 13 *Stanford Law & Policy Review* 33

Brown, R.L., "Activism is Not a Four-Letter Word" (2003) 73 *University Colorado Law Review* 1257

Callinan, I., "An Over-Mighty Court?" (1994) 4 *Proceedings of the Samuel Griffith Society* 81

Campbell E. and Groves M., "Attacks on Judges Under Parliamentary Privilege: A Sorry Australian Episode" [2002] *Public Law* 626

Campbell, T., "Judicial Activism—Justice of Treason?" (2003) 10 *Otago Law Review* 307

Cardozo, B., *The Nature of the Judicial Process* (Yale University Press, New Haven, 1921)

Carrigan, F., "A Blast from the Past: The Resurgence of Legal Formalism" (2003) 27 *Melbourne University Law Review* 163

Clayton, R., "The Limits of What's 'Possible': "Statutory Construction under the *Human Rights Act*" [2002] 5 *European Human Rights Law Review* 559

Coke, E., *Institute of the Lawes of England* (1628)

Cooke, R., "Fairness" (1989) 19 *University of Victoria Wellington Law Review* 421

Cooke, R., "The New Zealand National Legal Identity" (1987) 3 *Canterbury Law Review* 171

Cooke, R., *Turning Points of the Common Law* (47th Hamlyn Lectures, 1996) (Sweet & Maxwell, London, 1997)

Craven, G., "The High Court of Australia: A Study in the Abuse of Power" (1999) *University of New South Wales Law Journal* 216

Davies, M., "The Future of the Common Law: The Threat from Europe" (2003) 12:1 *Commonwealth Lawyer* 35

Davis, R. and Williams, G., "Reform of the Judicial Appointments Process; Gender and the Bench of the High Court of Australia" (2003) 27:3 *Melbourne University Law Review* 819

Dawson, D., "Intention and the Constitution—Whose Intent?" (1990) 6 *Australian Bar Review* 93

Denning, A., In *What Next in the Law* (Butterworths, London, 1982)

Denning, A., *Freedom Under the Law* (1st Hamlyn Lectures, 1949) (Stevens, London, 1949)

Devlin, P., "Judges and Lawmakers" (1976) 39 *Modern Law Review* 1

Devlin, P., "Judges, Government and Politics" (1978) 41 *Modern Law Review* 501

Diplock, W.J.K., "The Courts as Legislators" in *The Lawyer and Justice* (B. Harvey ed., Sweet and Maxwell, London, 1978)

Douglas, W.O., "Stare Decisis" (1949) 49 *Columbia Law Review* 735

Doyle, J., "Do Judges Make Policy? Should They?" (1998) 57 *Australian Journal of Public Administration* 89

Dworkin, R.W., *Taking Rights Seriously* (Duckworth, London, 1977)

Editorial, "Politicising High Court Appointments", *Courier Mail*, (Brisbane) March 10, 1997

Editorial, "A century of judicial independence" *The Advertiser* (Adelaide), October 10, 2003

Editorial, "A pillar of Australia's democratic life" *The Age* (Melbourne), October 9, 2003

Editorial, "Fischer sparks new High Court row" *The Age* (Melbourne), March 6, 1997

Elliott, D., "Conservative Judicial Activism Comes to Canada: *Egale v Canada* (2003) 36 *University of British Columbia Law Review* 29 at p. 42

Feeley, M.M. and Rubin E.L., *Judicial Policy Making and the Modern State: How the Courts Reformed America's Prisons* (Cambridge University Press, Cambridge, 1998)

Finkelstein, R., "Decision-making in a Vacuum?" (2003) 29 *Monash University Law Review* 11

Forte, D.F., *Natural Law and Contemporary Public Policy* (Georgetown University Press, 1998)

Frank, J., *Law and the Modern Mind* (Bretano's, New York, 1931)

Friendly, H.L. "The Courts and Social Policy: Substance and Procedure" in *Judges on Judging—Views from the Bench* (D. M. O'Brien ed., Chatham House, Chatham, 1997) 289

Gaille, S.S., "Publishing by US Court of Appeals Judges: Before and After the Bork Hearings" (1997) 26 *Journal of Legal Studies* 371

Galligan, B., *Politics of the High Court* (Uni Qld Press, 1987)

Gava, J., "Another Blast from the Past: Why the Left Should Embrace Strict Legalism" (2003) 27 *Melbourne University Law Review* 186

Gava, J., "The Rise of the Hero Judge" (2001) 24 *University of New South Wales Law Journal* 747

George, R.P., "Lincoln on Judicial Despotism", *First Things*, February 2003, 36

Gibb, F., "Blunkett v The Bench: The Battle has Begun", *The Times Online*, March 4, 2003

Gleeson, A.M., "Global Influences on the Australian Judiciary" (2002) 22 *Australian Bar Review* 184

Gleeson, A.M., "Individualised Justice: The Holy Grail" (1995) 69 *Australian Law Journal* 421

Gleeson, A.M., "Judicial Legitimacy" (2000) 20 *Australian Bar Review* 4

Gleeson, A.M., *The Rule of Law and the Constitution* (Boyer Lectures 2000) (Australian Broadcasting Commission, Sydney 2000)

Griffith, J.A.G., *The Politics of the Judiciary* (Fontana, London, 5th ed., 1997)

Guarnieri C. and Pederzoli P., *The Power of Judges—A Comparative Study of Courts and Democracy* (English ed. C. A. Thomas) (O.U.P., Oxford, 2002)

Handler, A.B., "Judging Public Policy" (2000) 31 *Rutgers Law Journal* 301

Hart Jr., H.M., and Sacks, A.M., *The Legal Process: Basic Problems in the Making and Application of Law* (Federation Press, Boston, 1994)

Hart, H.L.A., *The Concept of Law* (Clarendon Press, Oxford, 1961)

Hayne, K.M., "Letting Justice be Done Without the Heavens Falling" (2001) 27 *Monash University Law Review* 12

Henderson, G., "March of the High Court Murphyites" *Sydney Morning Herald*, February 1, 1992

Heraghty, B., "Defender of the Faith? The Role of the Attorney-General in Defending the High Court" (2002) 28 *Monash University Law Review* 206

Heydon, J.D., "Judicial Activism and the Death of the Rule of Law" (2003) 23:2 *Australian Bar Review* 110

Hirschl, R., "Resituating the Globalisation of Politics: *Bush v Gore* as a Global Trend" (2002) 15 *Canadian Journal of Law and Jurisprudence* 191

Holmes Jr., O.W., "The Path of the Law" (1897) 10 *Harvard Law Review* 457

Holmes Jr., O.W., *The Common Law* (1881) (Mark De Wolfe Howe ed., Macmillan, London, 1968)

Horrigan, B., "Paradigm Shifts in Judicial Interpretation: Reframing Legal and Constitutional Reasoning" in *Interpreting Constitutions—Theories, Principles and Institutions* (C. Sampford and K. Preston eds., Federation Press, Sydney, 1996)

Howard, C., "The High Court" (1994) 4 *Proceedings of the Samuel Griffith Society* 65

Hutchinson, A.C., "Heydon' Seek: Looking for Law in all the Wrong Places" (2003) 29 *Monash University Law Review* 85

Hutley, F.C., "The Legal Traditions of Australia as Contrasted with those of the United States" (1981) 55 *Australian Law Journal* 63

Ipp, D.A., "Judicial impartiality and judicial neutrality: Is there a difference?" (2000) 19 *Australian Bar Review* 212

Irvine, A.A.M., "The Impact of the *Human Rights Act*" [2003] *Public Law* 308

Judd, S., "The Unruly Horse Put Out to Pasture: The Doctrine of Public Policy in the Modern Law of Contract" (1996) 8 *Auckland University Law Review* 686

Justice, W.W., "Two Faces of Judicial Activism", *Judges on Judging—Views from the Bench* (D. M. O'Brien ed., Chatham House, Chatham, 1997)

Kelly J. and Murphy M., "Confronting Judicial Supremacy: A Defence of Judicial Activism and the Supreme Court of Canada's Legal Rights Jurisprudence" (2001) 16 *Canadian Journal of Law and Society* 3

Kennedy, *A Critique of Adjudication: Fin de Siecle* (Harvard University Press, Boston, 1997)

Kinslor, J., "'Killing Off' International Human Rights Law: An Exploration of the Australian Government's Relationship with United Nations Human Rights Committees" (2002) 8 *Australian Journal of Human Rights* 79

Kirby, M.D., "Attacks on Judges—A Universal Phenomenon" (1998) 72 *Australian Law Journal* 599

Kirby, M.D., "Challenges to Justice in a Plural Society" (2002) 11:2 *Commonwealth Lawyer* 35

Kirby, M.D., "Constitutional Interpretation and Original Intent: A Form of Ancestor Worship?" (2000) 24 *Melbourne University Law Review* 1

Kirby, M.D., "Courts and Policy: The Exciting Australian Scene" (1993) 19 *Commonwealth Law Bulletin* 1794

Kirby, M.D., "Judging: Reflections on the Moment of Decision" (1999) 18 *Australian Bar Review* 4

Kirby, M.D., "Judicial Activism" (1997) 27 *University of Western Australian Law Review* 1

Kirby, M.D., "Lord Cooke and Fundamental Rights" in *The Struggle for Simplicity in the Law—Essays for Lord Cooke of Thorndon* (P Rishworth ed., Butterworths, Wellington, 1997)

Kirby, M.D., "The Australian Use of International Human Rights Norms: From Bangalore to Balliol—A View from the

Antipodes" (1993) 16 *University of New South Wales Law Journal* 363

Kirby, M.D., "Towards a Grand Theory of Interpretation: The Case of Statutes and Contracts" (2003) 242 *Statute Law Review* 95

Kirby, M.D., *The Judges* (Boyer Lectures, 1983) (Australian Broadcasting Commission, Sydney, 1983)

Kirby, M.D., *Through the World's Eye* (Federation, Pyrmont, 2000)

Knight, W.S.M., "Public Policy in English Law" (1922) 38 *Law Quarterly Review* 207

Komesar, M.K., *Imperfect Alternatives* (University of Chicago Press, Chicago, 1994)

Kozlowski, M., *The Myth of the Imperial Judiciary* (N.Y.U. Press, New York, 2003)

Kumar, V., "Constitutional Democracy and Judicial Activism" in *India: 50 Years of Independence* (V. Grover and R. Arora eds., 1997)

Lane, C., "Republicans Investigate Judge in Michigan Case" *Washington Post*, November 1, 2003, A1

Lane, P., "Constitutional Implications and a Bill of Rights" (2001) 75 *Australian Law Journal* 469

Lasser, M., "Do Judges Deploy Policy?" (2001) 22 *Cardozo Law Review* 863

Lavarch, M., "How the High Court Considers Policy" (1998) *Australian Journal of Public Administration* 86

Learned Hand, B., Review (1922) 35 *Harvard Law Review* 479

Lewis, A., Foreword to M Kozlowski, *The Myth of the Imperial Judiciary* (N.Y.U. Press, New York, 2003)

Llewellyn, K., *The Common Law Tradition: Deciding Appeals* (Little Brown, Boston, 1960)

Llewellyn, K., *The Bramble Bush: On our Law and its Study* (Oceana, New York, 1951

Loveland, I., "Making it up as They Go Along? The Court of Appeal on Same-Sex Spouses and Succession Rights to Tenancies" [2003] *Public Law* 222

Lowi, T.I. "Policy at the Intersection of Law and Politics" unpublished keynote speech, 2 Symposium, Fall 2002 in *Cornell Journal of Law and Public Policy* (forthcoming)

Lowi, T.I., Review (1985) 63 *Texas Law Review* 1591

MacCormick, N., *Legal Reasoning and Legal Theory* (O.U.P., Oxford, 1978)

Maitland, F.W., Introduction, *Selden Society Year Book Series*, Vol 1

Malleson, K., "Assessing the Performance of the Judicial Services Commission" (1999) 116 *South African Law Journal* 36

Martin, F.F. (ed.) *International Human Rights Law and Practice* (Kluwer Law International, 1997)

Mason, A.F., "Changing the Law in a Changing Society" (1993) 67 *Australian Law Journal* 568

Mason, A.F., "Future Directions in Australian Law" (1987) 13 *Monash University Law Review* 149

Mason, A.F., "The Internationalisation of Domestic Law" Law and Policy Paper No. 4 (Centre for International and Public Law, Australian National University, Canberra, 1996)

Mason, A.F., "The Judge as Law-Maker" (1996) 3 *James Cook University Law Review* 1

Mason, A.F., "The Role of a Constitutional Court in a Federation: A Comparison of the Australian and the United States Experience" (1986) 16 *Federal Law Review* 1

Mason, A.F., "Foreword" in *The Principles of Equity*, (P. Parkinson ed., 2nd ed., LBC, Sydney, 2003)

McCluskey, J.H., *Law, Justice and Democracy* (*Reith Lectures*, 1987) (British Broadcasting Corporation, London, 1987)

McHugh, M.H. "The Law-Making Function of the Judicial Process—Part I" (1988) 62 *Australian Law Journal* 15

McHugh, M.H., "The Judicial Method" (1999) 73 *Australian Law Journal* 37

Meagher, D., "Guided by Voices? Constitutional Interpretation on the Gleeson Court" (2002) 7 *Deakin Law Review* 261

Merritt, C., "Court row as Williams vets judges", *Australian Financial Review*, December 11, 2002

Narayan, J., "Judicial Activism and Protection of Human Rights in India" (2001) 3 *Journal of Constitutional and Parliamentary Studies* 111

O'Dell E., (ed.), *Leading Cases of the Twentieth Century* (Round Hall, London, 2000)

Opeskin, B., "Constitutional Modelling: The Domestic Effect of International Law on Commonwealth Countries" (2001) 27 *Commonwealth Law Bulletin* 1242

Palley, C., *The United Kingdom and Human Rights* (43rd Hamlyn Lectures, 1990) (Sweet & Maxwell, London, 1991)

Parkinson, P., *Tradition and Change in Australian Law* (2nd ed., LBC, Sydney, 2001)

Patapan, H., "High Court Review, 2001: Politics, Legalism and the Gleeson Court" (2002) 37:2 *Australian Journal of Political Science* 241

Perry, J., "Have the Judges Gone Too Far?: Courts versus the People" (2003) 15:4 *Judicial Officers' Bulletin* (NSW) 25

Pierce, J.L., "Interviewing Australia's Senior Judiciary" (2002) 37 *Australian Journal of Political Science* 131

Plaxton, M., "The Formalist Conception of the Rule of Law and the *Marshall* Backlash" (2003) 8 *Review of Constitutional Studies* 66

Posner, R.A., *Overcoming Law* (Harvard University Press, Cambridge Mass., 1995)

Pound, R., *An Introduction to the Philosophy of Law*, (Storrs Lectures on Jurisprudence 1921–2) (Yale University Press, New Haven, 1922)

Pound, R., *Interpretations of Legal History* (C.U.P., Cambridge, 1923)

Presser, S.B., "What A Real Conservative Believes About 'Judicial Ideology'" (2003) 2d: 6 *The Green Bag* 285

Radcliffe, C. *The Law and Its Compass*, (Rosenthal Lectures, 1960) quoted in R. Stevens, *Law and Politics: The House of Lords as a Judicial Body 1800–1976* (Weidenfeld & Nicolson, London, 1979)

Radcliffe, C., *Not in Feather Beds* (Quality Book Club, London, 1968)

Raskin, J., *Overruling Democracy: The Supreme Court versus The American People* (Routledge, New York, 2003)

Reid, "The Judge as Lawmaker" (1972) 12 *Journal of Society of Public Teachers of Law* 23

Rishworth, P., "Lord Cooke and the Bill of Rights" in *The Struggle for Simplicity in the Law—Essays for Lord Cooke of Thorndon* (P. Rishworth ed., Butterworths, Wellington, 1997)

Robertson, D., *Judicial Discretion in the House of Lords* (Clarendon Press, Oxford, 1998)

Sackville, R., "Why Do Judges Make Law? Some Aspects of Judicial Law Making" (2001) 5 *University Western Sydney Law Review* 59

Savva, N., "Fischer seeks a more conservative court" *The Age* (Melbourne), March 5, 1997

Scalia, A., *A Matter of Interpretation: Federal Courts and the Law,* (Princeton University Press, Princeton, 1997)

Scarman, L.G., *English Law—The New Dimension* (26th Hamlyn Lectures, 1974) (Stevens, London, 1974)

Schubert, G., *Quantitative Analysis of Judicial Behaviour* (The Freer Press, New York, 1959)

Schubert, G., *The Judicial Mind* (Northwestern University Press, Evanston, 1965)

Sedley, S., "On Not Doing Anything for the First Time" (Atkin Lecture, November 6, 2001), at p. 3

Shearer, I., "United Nations Human Rights Committee: The *Toonen Case*" (1995) 69 *Australian Law Journal* 600

Smillie, J., "Formalism, Fairness and Efficiency: Civil Adjudication in New Zealand" [1996] *New Zealand Law Review* 254

Smyth, R., "Historical Consensual Norms in the High Court" (2001) 37 *Aust Journal of Political Science* 215

Solomon, D., "A Courtly Brawl", *Courier Mail*, February 27, 2003

Stapleton, J., "The Golden Thread at the Heart of Tort Law" (2003) 24:2 *Australian Bar Review* 135

Stevens, R., *The English Judges: Their Role in the Changing Constitution* (Hart Publishing, Oxford, 2002)

Steyn, J., "Democracy Through Law", (Robin Cooke Lecture, 2002) (2002) 6 *European Human Rights Law Review* 723

Steyn, J., "Does Legal Formalism Hold Sway in England?" (1996) 49 *Current Legal Problems* 43

Stone, H.F., "The Common Law in the United States" (1936) 50 *Harvard Law Review* 4

Stone, J., *Province and Function of Law* (Maitland, Sydney, 1946)

Stowe, H., "'The Unruly Horse' Has Bolted: *Tinsley v Milligan*" (1994) 57 *Modern Law Review* 441

Swearing in of Sir Owen Dixon as Chief Justice (1952) 85 C.L.R. xi

Symmons, C.R., "The Function and Effect of Public Policy in Contemporary Common Law" (1977) 51 *Australian Law Journal* 185

Tate, C.N. and Vallinder T. (eds.), *The Global Expansion of Judicial Power* (N.Y.U. Press, New York, 1995)

Taylor Jr., S., "The Last True Believer in Judicial Restraint" *The Atlantic Online*, April 23, 2002

Taylor, C., *Sources of the Self: The Making of the Modern Identity* (Harvard University Press, 1989)

Thayer, J.B., "The Origin and Scope of the American Doctrine of Constitutional Law" (1893) 7 *Harvard Law Review* 129

Thomas, E.W., "Fairness and Certainty in Adjudication: Formalism versus Substantialism" (1999) 9 *Otago Law Review* 459

Thomas, E.W., "Judging in the 21st Century" [2000] *New Zealand Law Journal* 228

Todd, S., "Negligence and Policy" in *The Struggle for Simplicity in the Law—Essays for Lord Cooke of Thorndon* (P. Rishworth ed., Butterworths, Wellington, 1997)

United Kingdom, Department for Constitutional Affairs, *Constitutional Reform: A Supreme Court for the United Kingdom*, Consultation Paper, Cmnd. 11/03 (2003)

Walker, J., "Judicial Tendencies in Statutory Construction: Differing Views on the Role of the Judge" (2001) 58 *New York University Annual Survey of American Law*, 2001 203

Waye, V., "Justiciability" in *Australian Studies in Law—Administrative Law* (M. Harris and V. Waye eds., Federation Press, Sydney, 1991)

White, G.E., "Felix Frankfurter's 'Soliloquy' in *Ex parte Quirin*" (2003) 2d: 5 *The Green Bag* 423

Winfield, P., "Public Policy in the English Common Law" (1929) 42 *Harvard Law Rev* 76

Winterton, G., "*Should the High Court consider Policy?*" (1998) *Australian Journal of Public Administration* 73

Woodward B., and Armstrong S., *The Brethren—Inside the Supreme Court* (Simon and Schuster, New York, 1979)

Woolf, H.K., "The International Role of the Judiciary", unpublished paper, Commonwealth Law Conference, Melbourne, April 2003

Wright, "The Study of Law" (1938) 54 L.Q.R. 185

Yeats, W.B., "The Lake Isle of Innisfree" in W B Yeats, *Collected Poems*, (Macmillan, London, 1982)

Young, E.A., "Judicial Activism and Conservative Politics" (2002) 73 *University of Colorado Law Review* 1139

Young, J., "The Constitutional Limits of Judicial Activism: Judicial Conduct of International Relations and Child Abduction" (2003) 66 *Modern Law Review* 823

Zander, M., *The State of Justice* (51st Hamlyn lectures, 1999) (Sweet & Maxwell, London, 2000)

Zeigler, D.H., "The New Activist Court" (1996) 45 *American University Law Review* 1367

Zines, L., "Judicial Activism and the Rule of Law in Australia" in *Judicial Power, Democracy and Legal Positivism* (T. Campbell and J. Goldsworthy eds., Aldershot, Ashgate, 2000)

Zines, L., "Legalism, Realism and Judicial Rhetoric in Constitutional Law" (Byers Lecture) (2002) *N.S.W. Bar Notes* 13

INDEX

Index

Index

Index

United States—*cont.*
    judicial creativity, 15
    judicial nomination hearings,
        71
    judicial writing, reduction in,
        47
    judiciary, attacks on, 47
    legal positivism, 15
    literalism, 39
    public policy, 20
    slavery, 67–68
    US Constitution, interpretation
        of, 4–5, 39, 45
Universal Declaration of Human
    Rights, 75

Values
    common law, 83
    personal, 29
    shared, 17
    societal, 82–83

Warren, Chief Justice Earl, 71
Wright, Lord, 14

Year Books, 4, 21

Zines, Leslie, 36, 40–41, 50, 52